HANDBOOK for the HEART
Original Writings on Love

Edited by

RICHARD CARLSON

and

BENJAMIN SHIELD

Foreword by
JOHN GRAY

BACK BAY BOOKS

LITTLE, BROWN AND COMPANY
Boston New York Toronto London

P9-DFZ-638

This book is dedicated to you, the reader.
May your life be filled with love.

Also edited by
RICHARD CARLSON AND BENJAMIN SHIELD
Healers on Healing
For the Love of God
Handbook for the Soul

BY RICHARD CARLSON
You Can Be Happy No Matter What
You Can Feel Good Again
Shortcut Through Therapy
Don't Sweat the Small Stuff

Copyright © 1996 by Richard Carlson and Benjamin Shield

All rights reserved. No part of this book may be reproduced in any form
or by any electronic or mechanical means, including information storage
and retrieval systems, without permission in writing from the publisher,
except by a reviewer who may quote brief passages in a review.

Originally published in hardcover by Little, Brown and Company, 1996
First Back Bay Paperback edition, 1998

Library of Congress Cataloging-in-Publication Data

Handbook for the heart : original writings on love/edited by Richard Carlson
and Benjamin Shield ; foreword by John Gray. — 1st ed.
    p.   cm.
  ISBN 978-0-316-12004-3   0-316-12004-9 (pb)
  1. Love. 2. Love — Religious aspects.
 I. Carlson, Richard. II. Shield, Benjamin.
BD436.H26 1996
128'.4 — dc20   96-12168

Published simultaneously in Canada by Little, Brown & Company
(Canada) Limited

Printed in the United States of America

CONTENTS

Acknowledgments

We offer our gratitude to the following people for their loving assistance in the creation of this book:

Jennifer Josephy and Little, Brown and Company, for their shared belief in our vision.

Patti Breitman, Sheree Bykofsky, and Linda Michaels, for their professionalism and enthusiasm.

Stephen Lamont for his excellent copyediting.

Gay Edelman, Barry Fox, Dr. Pamela DuMond-Shield, Tom Bedell, Mark Lipsman, Steve Hasenberg, and Valerie Harms, for their imagination and dedication.

We especially wish to offer our appreciation and respect to all the participants who shared their wisdom and so freely gave of their heart. They remind us that the best way to teach is to show by example. Our heartfelt thanks to all who were involved with this project.

Foreword

BY *John Gray, Ph.D.*

LOVE HAS BECOME the Holy Grail of our time. People want more of it, suffer from lack of it, and search for it all their lives. This book, *Handbook for the Heart*, dwells on this quest for love and provides the skills we need on our path. In these pages the leading practitioners on matters of the heart examine the many facets of the diamond of love, enabling us to fulfill our deepest longings.

For many of us the difficulty in our relationships is because we have had to adjust to a cultural transition from an old form of coupling to a new way. In the past, people sought marriage partners primarily to create a family and to ensure security. Men worked outside the home; women raised the children. Both parents expected the children to help with the work and take care of them when they were old. Now, however, men and women are more self-sufficient and less dependent on each other for security and survival. Men can raise children, and women hold jobs. As a result, men and women increasingly seek out each other to fulfill long-denied emotional needs.

Therefore, the basis for marriage has changed. We marry not for survival but for the satisfactions of intimacy. Ironically, the reason for so many divorces today is that people want more love, not less. Many feel that their desires for love must be met in order to stay with their partners.

We yearn to feel loved, admired, and appreciated, not just leaned on for financial security. Once people are able to support their families, they can then focus on the quality of their shared connection. New meaning and purpose in life emerges in establishing heartfelt bonds. *Handbook for the Heart* helps you remove the blocks to achieving deep loving relationships.

To attain such love, we must be sensitive to the love we need and know how to get it, as well as how to give the love our partners need. Thus, we must have better forms of communication than those used by our parents. We have to be able to articulate those needs as both we and our partners change over the course of time. It used to be that men and women lived in different worlds, without even attempting to share their innermost thoughts and feelings. My mother, for example, never expected my dad to be a great conversationalist.

Today, men and women have to learn how to negotiate with respect. In today's world, men are no longer responsible for simply one area, e.g., the budget, and women another, e.g., the social schedule. As women are earning more of the income needed to raise a family, they want to have more of a say in how the money is spent. And men want to participate in the planning of their leisure time. The ascendance of love in our relationships also creates a greater capacity for romance and the nurturing of children.

Again, in the past the concept of love was different: a sense of caring grew out of loyalty and shared history. Romance was not important or expected to endure. It was considered loving to sacrifice yourself for your partner. Today, people are no longer willing to stay together in a life of sacrifice. If we sacrifice who we are in a relationship, we lose touch with ourselves and our feelings. To us, loving means passion, partnership, romance, and good communication. Feelings have become enormously significant. Love, intimacy, and closeness are more important than ever before.

To fill my own life with love, I prioritize and carry out the most important acts that create love. In my marriage I've learned it's usually the little things that make a difference. My wife and I have loving rituals, things we do that the other appreciates. For example, when I'm driving my car with my wife, I always slow down at yellow lights and stop. She's grateful because she knows that when I'm driving alone, I often run yellow lights. I'll even say to her, "I did that for you, honey." She usually replies with a chuckle and says, "Thank you very much." Another example is that, even after ten years of marriage, I still bring home fresh-cut flowers. It's the little things that keep romance alive.

With my children, I make sure that I create plenty of uninterrupted time with them when we're doing fun things. I've taught my children that if they need my full attention when I'm busy, they can always pull on my pant leg and I will stop what I'm doing to listen to them. Also, when I travel, I remember to bring them back something from my trip — a tiny token, anything, to make them feel special.

The little things that say "I care" are the most effective in filling a life with love.

One way I make sure to get my own emotional needs met is to take time for activities that I enjoy. Even when my wife thinks we need quality time together, if I'm not in the right mood, I take time to be alone — although I assure her that later we can have our time together, too. When we give to ourselves first, we have more to give to our relationships and family.

So many people, under the illusion of being nice, sacrifice too much of who they are and thus lose their ability to truly love and get the love they need. People suffer from not realizing how vital love is to them. Love is an essential vitamin, especially in a society that emphasizes efficiency, productivity, and virtual reality. Many times the absence of love causes our frustrations, anxieties, illnesses, and fatigue. People don't realize what they are missing.

Handbook for the Heart offers a refuge from the busyness of life and illuminates the joys to be gained from love. To read this book, to hear the words of people who have made it their life's work to define what love is, to articulate how we can most successfully express, give, and receive love, is of immense value — and an extraordinary gift. *Handbook for the Heart* will affect your life in innumerable positive ways, as it has mine.

Introduction

*"It is only with the heart that one can see rightly; what
is essential is invisible to the eye."*

— SAINT-EXUPÉRY (1900–44)

The Little Prince

IF YOU WERE GIVEN one wish for our world, what would it be? Ours would be, quite simply, that each and every one of us could feel at peace. And we believe that the gift of peace begins with hearts filled with love.

Who among us does not desire more love in our lives? And who among us hasn't sighed, and pushed ahead with the busyness of our day and our lives, letting the opportunities of love slip away? A hug from a child is shortened to take a phone call, a friend is seldom contacted because of distance, a compliment from a mate goes unacknowledged for a question about a bill, a favorite charity is pushed to the back of our minds for "later." It seems the truly important, heart-connecting moments are so often neglected. And our lives, all of our lives, are made smaller.

We know we want and need love, to both give and receive in full measure. But how do we slow down and allow more love into our lives, when inner and outer pressures detract us from our heart's deepest desire? There are many extraordinary individuals who have dedicated their lives to answering just that question. With the knowledge that such role models exist, we asked them directly for specific and practical advice and guidelines on filling our lives with love. "How," we asked them, "do you do it?"

So, the idea for this book was born. We created a "wish list" of possible participants, individuals who have been teaching us — and much of the world — about love for many years. People who have earned the reputation as experts on love. Sometimes we had doubts. Would these wonderful teachers be willing to share their knowledge in an original, single compilation? In the end, though, we let our willingness to take the chance and our need to know rule, and we went forward. We invited each teacher to discuss his or her own way of filling life with love. Almost without exception, the individuals we approached agreed to share their wisdom and insights into why we need to fill our lives with love and, most important, how we can do it.

We were rewarded beyond our greatest imagination. The depth of sincerity of each of the participants is overwhelming. We saw, up close, how each contributor makes an honest and true effort to "walk her walk," to "practice what he preaches." Never before have we met and worked with individuals so completely and sincerely dedicated to a loving existence. The peaceful spiritual leader Mahatma Gandhi once said, "My life is my message." We believe that the same thing is true for each of the participants in this book. Each of them, in a unique and personal way, tells us with certainty how the heart is the fundamental source of our connection with all of life.

Love — giving and receiving from the heart — involves compassion, stillness, gratitude, peace, intimacy and relationship with others, and service. From the perspective of the authors of this collection, love is the only true measure of our success in life. Nothing else ultimately matters. As Mother Teresa is quoted in one of the articles, "We cannot do great things. We can only do small things with great love."

Creating this small thing, this original anthology, is for us an act of great love — for ourselves, for each other, for our families, and for you, our readers. We'd like to thank all the contributors for the richness they have contributed to our own lives and to the lives of so many millions. This project, these writings — these people — have changed and enriched our own lives in profound and remarkable ways. We wish this, most of all, for you — that you, too, will find new ways to bring love into your life and that you find the peace a love-filled heart brings.

From the heart,

BENJAMIN SHIELD, PH.D.
RICHARD CARLSON, PH.D.

1.

The Power
of the Heart

"That best portion of a good man's life,
His little, nameless, unremembered acts
Of kindness and of love."

— WILLIAM WORDSWORTH (1770–1850)

THE POWER OF
LOVING-KINDNESS

BY *Sharon Salzberg*

"There is a saying in the Buddhist tradition: 'You can explore the universe looking for somebody who is more deserving of your love and affection than you are yourself, and you will not find that person anywhere.'"

THE POWER OF love or loving-kindness has been denigrated in our culture. There's a sense that a loving person is abused, allows tyranny to reign without protest, and isn't strong. It's almost a sense that love is a weakness. Sometimes there is the idea that the loving heart makes people kind of smirky and sentimental—that because of love, they can't look at suffering clearly or at difficult things within themselves or in the world. I think we have to do a radical re-visioning and come to understand the power of the loving heart. Not only is it innate, but it cannot be destroyed, no matter what our life experience has been, no matter how many scars we bear, how much suffering we have gone through, or how

3

unloved we have felt. We have the capacity to love and to receive love in return.

Living in fear is like being frozen. It's said that the Buddha taught love — particularly *metta,* loving-kindness — as the antidote to fear. There is a beautiful line in a poem by Mary Oliver: "When the thumb of fear lifts, we are so alive." We're oppressed by our fears, our judgments, our guilt — guilt being considered in the Buddhist psychology a quality of self-hatred — and when that oppression lifts, we are so alive. That's the force of love.

Sometimes, if we're fortunate, we experience this love with another person. We might have one being in our life who is a model of unconditional love, so that we don't fear rejection if we're truly honest with this person or if we don't present ourselves in a certain way. We have enormous respect for this person, who means safety and maybe clarity — not mushiness or a phony veneer or an inability to look at difficult and painful things. This person may perceive the difficulty and pain in us, but there is the feeling that he or she views them alongside us, rather than from across some enormous gulf of separation. That is really the essence of a loving heart — the understanding of our nonseparateness.

There is a saying in the Buddhist tradition: "You can explore the universe looking for somebody who is more deserving of your love and affection than you are yourself, and you will not find that person anywhere." We ourselves are as deserving of our love and affection as anyone else. A spiritual practice based on self-hatred can never sustain itself. We have to begin with loving ourselves, being able to embrace all parts of ourselves as well as all parts of the world, in order to understand our capacity to love.

The Buddha said, "If you truly loved yourself, you would never harm another." Harming another is like harming ourselves. Buddhist psychology distinguishes between the force of guilt and the force of remorse — remorse being a full consciousness and sensitivity that we've hurt somebody. Feeling that pain, we let go and then have the energy to move on. Guilt is something else entirely — a continual rehashing of some event, mental flagellation, with tremendous self-hatred. It leaves us strained and exhausted, without the energy to go on and be different.

If self-judgment, criticism, and self-hatred were liberating, we would all have been freed long ago. I don't have anything against those mind states personally — except that they simply don't work. Don't get me wrong; I don't have a philosophical stance that we have to love ourselves, but the fact is, love works and hatred doesn't. Self-hatred may not arise from anything in particular — it may just be a sense of personal humiliation about the fact that we grow older, get sick or disabled, feel that we failed, get angry, or get jealous. We can easily hate, judge, and condemn, but unfortunately, it doesn't end the problems — in some strange way, it intensifies them.

The Buddha said, "Develop a mind so filled with love, it resembles space." We use the words *mind* and *heart* synonymously; the meaning is to develop a heart so filled with love that it resembles space, which can't be marred, can't be ruined — just as if someone were standing in a room throwing paint around in the air. There's nowhere in space for the paint to land. We can develop a mind or heart so filled with love that it's like space — boundless, open, vast, free. Any amount of paint, any irritant, any inner or outer trouble, won't land.

Recently I was in Israel teaching a forgiveness meditation. During the session, someone said he had survived a terrorist attack — he still had some bullets in his body and was in constant pain. He said he didn't think it was possible to forgive, but he did know it was essential to learn to stop hating.

It's clear that if we don't stop hating, nobody will. It has to start with us because not only are we ourselves suffering horribly from the limitation and burning of all that anger, but the world is never going to change unless one person somewhere starts to stop hating.

We develop a loving heart by some form of meditation practice, a process distinct from reading about something or admiring it in a distant way. By meditating for even five minutes a day on a pragmatic level, so that it's not theoretical or even devotional, we can see for ourselves, "What happens when I say this phrase or do this reflection on everybody wanting to be happy? What happens when I sit down for five minutes and wish myself love and safety and peace? What happens when I think of this person I care about so much and am grateful to, or when I think of somebody I really don't like and reflect on the fact that he or she also wants to be happy?" It's an experiment.

Sometimes people feel odd — when they undertake a practice of a loving heart — they think it's artificial and it seems mechanical, but in fact, it's not. I often use the example of planting seeds through harnessing the force of our intention, like planting our garden of love. It will definitely blossom, but we have to take those first steps, to risk or be willing to explore what kind of development can occur in the loving heart.

One technique I like is developing *metta* toward a neutral person. It's interesting because sometimes we have difficulty finding a neutral person. As soon as we think of someone, we have an instant judgment about liking or disliking this person. That's an important revelation. It lets us see that we have an enormous number of neutral people in our lives on whom we've imposed judgments. This can come as a shock to us. It's interesting to consider someone about whom we have no story — just a generic living being, wanting to be happy, like all of us — and offering the same care and cherishing we've just offered ourselves and perhaps someone we love deeply. A sense of separation falls away. Some people, in intensive *metta* during a retreat, contemplate a neutral person and actually have the feelings of falling in love! Not romantically, but in terms of a loving friendship.

One of the tremendous understandings of spiritual practice is the power of the mind. Although we all live in the same world, our individual reality is a function not only of external events but of how they're held in our hearts — the degree of space in our hearts, the vastness or constriction, the contraction or openness of the mind receiving the external events. The spiritual perspective is not that we're sitting in traffic and are really angry and are trying to pretend we're not. Instead, it's an openness to what we're actually feeling; to understanding suffering; to having a great deal of love, kindness, and compassion for ourselves — not being stuck in that first reaction of anger. It's having options, choices — which is what an open heart means, as opposed to a narrow one — and realizing we can look at matters a different way.

In *Lovingkindness,* I tell a story about my friend Sylvia Boorstein being on a plane that developed a problem with its hydraulic system. It had to return to the airport, and every five minutes the pilot would announce the countdown over the PA system, "Thirty-five minutes left to land . . . thirty minutes left to land." The whole time, Sylvia was consciously doing a loving-kindness practice for the people in her immediate family, enveloping them with care and concern and acknowledging her connection to all of them. When the pilot got on the PA system and said, "We have five minutes before we land," Sylvia realized that in five minutes she might be dead. She resumed her loving-kindness practice and found there was no way in the world she could limit herself to opening her heart to just her immediate family. The only thing she could do at that moment, when she might have only five minutes to live, was to open her heart to all beings everywhere. This was without any contrivance or force or pretentiousness.

Metta is not a fabricated decision like "Now I am a very spiritual person and therefore I will love all beings"; nor does it mean that if we're really seething with rage or filled with fear, we're somehow going to overlay a nice little veneer and pretend and be smiling all the time. It's not that at all. *Metta* is the moment Sylvia had when the sense of "us and them" crumbled. It was born of the understanding that she might soon be dead — so why bother upholding all those boundaries and barriers? With the collapse of those boundaries, the effortless, natural love for all beings wells up. That's the moment we look for. That's the moment when we are so alive.

Our practice shows us our own strength. Very early on, one of my teachers said something wonderful to me: "The Buddha's enlightenment solved the Buddha's problems; now you solve yours." Our practice shows us that "I do have the wisdom, I do have the strength, I do have the loving capacity, in real-time, real-life situations, to look at things in a different way." That's what our practice gives us.

HEART SOUNDS

BY *Deepak Chopra, M.D.*

"The way to fill your life with love is very simple: if you want more love, give more love."

FILLING OUR LIVES with love is so important because love is the only true reality. Ultimately, whatever we're doing in life, we do because we are seeking love. Love is God. It is the experience of the sacred. Everything we do, we do for love. Someone once said, "The Nobel laureates are looking for love. The award is but a consolation prize." Since there is nothing else that really matters, it behooves us all to make love the true priority in our lives. We need to recognize the importance of love and we need to do so not just with lip service but by integrating love into our very being.

Love is the ultimate experience because all forms of love are expressions of God. People often think about love as an emotion or a sentiment. But love is so much more! Deep emotions and sentiments can be extremely nurturing, yes. But love is truly the ultimate reality. It is the experience of unity consciousness — meaning that the observer and the observed are experienced as one, the seer and the scenery are experienced as one, the lover and the beloved are experienced as one. Love is the experiential knowledge that we are all the same being: we are all one. We only appear in different disguises; our essential nature is shared. And it is the awareness of our essential nature that allows us to give and receive love freely.

When you have this experiential knowledge of unity consciousness, this profound understanding that we are all one, you become unable to hurt others or to be hurt. Instead, there is only love, ecstasy, and joy. Saint Augustine said, "I'm in love with loving." When you ask, "What is the purpose of love?" the answer is "There is no purpose." Love is its own reward. And the more love you give, the more love you receive. In fact, when the love is unconditional and from the heart, the return is directly proportional to the giving. You receive as much as you give. And so the way to fill your life with love is very simple: if you want more love, give more love.

You see, the universe operates through dynamic exchange; giving and receiving are merely different aspects of the energy flow in the universe. As we decide to give what we also seek — love — we keep the flow of love circulating in our lives and in the world. In offering love to others, we ensure that there is always plenty for ourselves. As long as we are giving love, there is no need to worry about getting enough. It will come. It comes the moment that we offer love to another, because receiving is the same as giving. They are simply two different aspects of the flow of energy in the universe.

There are specific ways you can participate in the energy flow. Humans have three profound needs: appreciation, attention, and affection. Attending to these needs brings more love into your life on a day-to-day, moment-to-moment basis.

Appreciation means telling others that you care for and treasure them. It's important to express this appreciation as often as you can. I try my best to find something special to honor and admire in every human being I encounter. I think it's only right to tell people what I see. My action satisfies my need to appreciate as well as their need to be appreciated.

Attention is the ability to listen with the totality of your being. It means taking the time to be truly present to others instead of being distracted by your own thoughts or letting your mind wander. In my own life, I try my best to be fully present, whether I'm with a waitress, someone who asks a question at one of my lectures, a family member, someone I work with, a friend, or someone on the other end of the phone. The other person deserves my undivided attention. And when I offer it, both of us are served.

Affection is touching somebody in a loving manner. It means showing someone, in an open, loving way, that I care for him or her. Showing affection, with gentle gestures and touches, is a wonderful way to fill your life with love. A simple handclasp, a light stroking, a big bear hug keep the energy of love flowing in both people's lives.

Messages about loving come to us from our hearts as well as from our bodies. I recognize that both my heart and my body are very intelligent sources that allow me to make karmically correct choices, choices that are governed by love rather than by rationality. I have learned not to trust my intellect over my heart. In a business situation, for example, my intellect or rational mind may tell me that something is not a good idea. It might say, "Don't do it," but my heart might say, "You should do it." In these cases I always follow my heart. I believe that the best decisions — karmically correct decisions — are always made from a place of love.

My best advice is this. With every encounter, with every single human being you meet, ask yourself one simple question: "What can I give this person?" Don't be concerned with what you can get back, but focus entirely on what you can do for him or her. And what you do can be quite simple. When I go to someone's home, for example, I often bring a small gift or pick a flower. What you give doesn't have to be something material. There is always something you can offer, and the giving is always very powerful. You can say something nice, or even silently wish the person happiness or some other type of goodwill. Even the thought of blessing someone, sending loving thoughts, or giving a simple silent prayer has the power to affect others.

If you start bringing love into your life, consciously and deliberately filling your life with love, you begin to see miracles all around you. Your life becomes an expression of love, and you see things you never thought possible happening in both your inner and your outer life. If you strive to give love, all else begins to come to you.

By participating in the flow of love in the universe, we can affect the whole world. We are the world! The outer world is but an expression of our inner world. Whatever is happening in our inner world is reflected "out there." The so-called criminals of society, deluded dreamers, the misfits, are nothing other than projections of our collective shadow-self. Once we confront this truth, we realize that there is no sense in trying to go out and change the world. If we would just change ourselves, the world would transform and take care of itself.

It is easy, so easy, to get distracted and say, "Oh, my God, look at all the bad that's happening in the world." But we can't give in to that notion; we have to keep our focus on the love. There does seem to be a newfound acceptance in the idea of a critical mass, a definite change in the collective psyche of the world, as more and more people make love a priority. Real change is happening. By giving love, always love, we can continue to influence what happens in the rest of the world. If enough of us embrace love, the world will eventually be saturated with love. The love in the world begins with the love within ourselves.

The Heart Is
Always Open

By *Stephen and Ondrea Levine*

"People say life is so short. That isn't true at all. Life is so long that we don't have a moment to waste without forgiveness and loving-kindness. Life is so long that without spiritual practice, very few people are alive enough to die on their deathbeds. Most people have died years and years before."

JUST AS THE sun is always shining, the heart is always open. We don't need to do anything to be more loving except let go of what blocks the natural luminescence of the heart. Being more loving is a process of watching the fears and desires that make us unloving. To be truly loving means living in the present — not in the past or in the future — and trying to meet even the closed heart with kindness.

Of course, there are distractions — there's a lot of noise out there in a world of gluttony and ambition. But nothing outside can pull us from our center. Desire pulls from within. We're simply fishing — for delights, for safety, for pride. We can't blame the fish for our interest and excitement in catching them! I think it was Hari Dass who said that one of his most profound recognitions was the element of suffering that is in pleasure. We hold on to pleasure, desiring to prolong its impermanence, and the rope that burns as it's dragged beyond our grasp. If we work on our own desire system — if we remove our hooks from the water — then fish become a beautiful thing. Instead of carp for our plates, they become something we can sit and watch, like koi, those large Japanese goldfish. Just as our perception of the fish swimming in the water is altered, our relationship to the objects of our desires changes radically. Desire then isn't what draws us out of ourselves; it becomes what re-minds us as it arises. It becomes something that opens our heart, because nothing opens the heart like watching what closes it, distracts it, dilutes it, or confuses it.

Our conditioning came about from continuous building, and we free ourselves the same way: a moment of mercy here, a millisecond of forgiveness there. These flashes may seem like so little, but people come to us all the time and say, "You know, if I'm going to be truthful, I'd have to say my heart's open maybe two minutes a week." They're really concerned, and we laugh — we almost swoon. We tell them, "In this world, on this plane of suffering, it's a miracle that the heart is open at all." But that it doesn't happen all at once is good, because none of us, almost none of us, is prepared for the enormity of our great heart — we'd pass out.

People do all this arduous spiritual work to understand the great heart of the divine. When we get there, we discover that nothing has any meaning in itself; all meaning is added by the mind. The only rational act of a lifetime is love. When we get to the great truth, nothing makes any sense but love. The rest of it was just the confusion we created to avoid suffering. Love gives us an opportunity to let go into the enormity, the very source of satisfaction, which is our true nature and which we merely glimpse each time we fulfill a desire. In that millisecond when desire is absent, we experience what we call satisfaction. This is not because the desire was fulfilled, but because the nature of satisfaction is a parting of the clouds, a moment when desire is absent from the mind and when love expresses itself effortlessly, naturally, radiantly.

People say to us, "If I could just find the right mate, I'd be happy the rest of my life." That's being drawn out by desires, by the fishhook in the water. A relationship does not in itself make us happy. Nothing makes us happy except the work we do inside, because we're only truly happy when our heart is open. But relationships are a forum for that inner work. Nothing teaches us how unloving we are like relationships do. They put us in a position where we're confronted daily with our holding, our fears, our expectations, our anger, our distrust. In the world — even in the meditation hall or the monastery — we can participate on our own terms. We can meditate when we want, pray when we want. If an untoward thought or feeling arises, no one knows it but us. We can keep up the pretense of being a person who loves God. But in a relationship we can't do that. All pretenses eventually burst into flames and destroy the structural integrity of the relationship.

The difficulties in relationships are one of their most precious gifts — provided we have a partner with whom we can let go and not be abused for letting go. As we become more spiritual, one of the difficulties is that we may have a tendency to stay in a bad relationship because we think that it's good for our personal development. That's a tricky one. The idea that we can't be a good person unless we can be abused does not help the world. Letting ourselves be abused is not an act of compassion; it may actually be an act of self-righteousness. The difficulty with relationships is either that fear keeps us from committing or that we commit blindly and are caught by our own desires and expectations. If our partners are what we love most in the world, we and our partners are in big trouble. If our partners are the *people* we love most in the world, and if God or the truth — whatever we choose to call it — is what we love most, then the relationship with those people is our most profound desire.

People say life is so short. That isn't true at all. Life is so long that we don't have a moment to waste without forgiveness and loving-kindness. Life is so long that without spiritual practice, very few people are alive enough to die on their deathbeds. Most people have died years and years before. We've sold off a spiritual arm, a spiritual leg. We've denied so many parts of our true nature, so many parts of our heart — it's phenomenal how much we have died. Death isn't the problem; the problem is how dead we lived — how little the priority of the heart has motivated us; how much, day to day, we have tripped and fallen headlong into another unconscious moment, seeing someone else as the object of the mind instead of as the subject of the heart.

Relationships give us continual opportunities to be aware. People hold pieces of silk over their heads and jump out of airplanes, calling it skydiving, or jump off bridges while attached to bungee cords. When asked, "Why do you do these dangerous sports?" they say, "Because it makes me feel so alive." When we're trying to survive, all our awareness is brought to that situation. Where our awareness is, there's our aliveness. Usually our awareness is diffuse, like the sun on a winter day. But, as with the sun on a winter day, we can focus awareness through a magnifying glass and put a blazing pinpoint of light where we want it.

A relationship does the same thing. Relationships are the ultimate danger sport because, moment to moment, we don't know whether we'll survive—whether our self-image will emerge intact. Ideally, it won't! The more intact our self-image, the more isolated we are from the enormity of the truth. The more we let go of our fears, the more we can let go of our expectations and be concerned about whether the other person is feeling loved instead of whether we are feeling loved. As Saint Francis said, "It's time to love instead of looking to be loved." If we love, we'll be more loved than we ever imagined. Nothing is more sublime than an open heart.

VALUING LOVE

BY *Nathaniel Branden, Ph.D.*

"How do I bring love into my life? My answer is that I focus day after day principally on what I care most about in this world—on what I most respect and admire. That is what I give my time and attention to."

I DO NOT KNOW if there has ever been a time in history when the word *love* has been used so promiscuously as it is at present.

We are told constantly that we must "love" everyone. Leaders of movements declare that they "love" followers they have never met. Enthusiasts of personal-growth workshops and encounter-group weekends emerge from such experiences announcing that they "love" all people everywhere.

Just as a currency, in the process of becoming more and more inflated, has less and less purchasing power, so words, through an analogous process of inflation, through being used less and less discriminately, are progressively emptied of meaning.

It is possible to feel benevolence and goodwill toward human beings one does not know or does not know very well. It is not possible to feel love. Aristotle made this observation twenty-five hundred years ago, and we still need to remember it. In forgetting it, all we accomplish is the destruction of the concept of love.

Love by its very nature entails a process of selection, of discrimination. Love is our response to what represents our highest values. Love is a response to distinctive characteristics possessed by some beings but not by all. Otherwise, what would be the tribute of love?

If love between adults does not imply admiration, if it does not imply an appreciation of traits and qualities that the recipient of love possesses, what meaning or significance would love have and why would anyone consider it desirable?

In his book *The Art of Loving*, Erich Fromm wrote: "In essence, all human beings are identical. We are all part of One; we are One. This being so, it should not make any difference whom we love."

Really? If we were to ask our lovers why they care for us, consider what our reaction would be if told, "Why shouldn't I love you? All human beings are identical. Therefore, it doesn't make any difference whom I love. So it might as well be you." Not very inspiring, is it?

So I find the advocacy of "universal love" puzzling—if one takes words literally. Not everyone condemns sexual promiscuity, but I have never heard of anyone who hails it as an outstanding virtue. But *spiritual* promiscuity? Is *that* an outstanding virtue? Why? Is the spirit so much less important than the body?

In commenting on this paradox, Ayn Rand wrote in *Atlas Shrugged:* "A morality that professes the belief that the values of the spirit are more precious than matter, a morality that teaches you to scorn a whore who gives her body indiscriminately to all men — the same morality demands that you surrender your soul in promiscuous love for all comers."

My own impression is that people who talk of "loving" everyone are, in fact, expressing a wish or a plea that everyone love them. But to take love — above all, love between adults — *seriously,* to treat the concept with respect and distinguish it from generalized benevolence or goodwill, is to appreciate that it is a unique experience possible between some people but not between all.

Consider the case of romantic love. When two adults with significant spiritual and psychological affinities encounter each other, and if they have evolved to a decent level of maturity — if they are beyond the level of merely struggling to make their relationship "work" — then romantic love can become a pathway, not only to sexual and emotional happiness but also to higher reaches of human growth. It can become a context for a continuing encounter with the self, through the process of interaction with another self. Two consciousnesses, each dedicated to personal evolution, can provide an extraordinary stimulus and challenge to each other.

But such a possibility presupposes self-esteem. The first love affair we must consummate successfully is with ourselves; only then are we ready for a relationship with another. A person who feels unworthy and unlovable is not ready for romantic love.

Of course, there are other kinds of love besides romantic love. What I feel for my grandchildren is a different kind of love. What it has in common with romantic love, however, is that I see in my grandchildren values and traits that touch my heart. But it would be a corruption of language to say that I "love" my grandchildren the same as I "love" children whom I do not even know. Whatever my feelings for other children, the experience is entirely different.

Apart from what I feel for my wife, Devers — who is the highest value in my life — writing is my paramount passion. What this means, practically, is that a good deal of my time and energy is devoted to writing. This has to do with *living* one's values, not simply professing them.

You ask, "How do I bring love into my life?" My answer is that I focus day after day principally on what I care most about in this world — on what I most respect and admire. That is what I give my time and attention to.

Since my highest priorities are my marriage and my work, I give the greatest part of my time and energy to them. With regard to my wife, I frequently communicate to her my awareness of all the traits and characteristics in her that I so much love, respect, appreciate, and admire.

We all want to be seen, understood, appreciated. I call this the need for the experience of psychological visibility. I strive to make my wife feel visible to me.

I also spend a great deal of time thinking about the things I love. I am keenly aware of how much there is in my life to appreciate and enjoy. I dwell on that every day. I do not take anything good in my life for granted.

I am always aware of our mortality. I know that if I love someone, the time to express it is today. If I value something, the time to honor it is today.

THE BEST-KEPT SECRET

BY *Barry Neil Kaufman*

"If perceptions lead to behaviors, can our thoughts bring love into our lives? Absolutely. I know for a fact that we can make the choice to love, that we can make that choice come alive, and that it's sustainable, renewable, and ever-deepening."

I FINALLY HAPPENED UPON a simple definition of love that has allowed me to activate it in my life in ways that astound me. My definition is threefold: love is accepting and nonjudgmental; love is wanting the best for another person; and love is doing something useful to help another person realize his or her potential.

An initial awareness that has been a guiding point and beacon in my life, and one that may actually be the best-kept secret on this planet, is simply this: love is a choice. I never realized this as I was growing up. Instead, it almost seemed to me that love fell out of the sky and hit you on the head or was otherwise magically manifested. And I believe that this idea is not an uncommon one. In our culture, love is viewed as a passive experience, something that just "happens to you." We see love more as a reaction than an action, and we have systematically learned to become wallflowers in the dance of love. Even the way we speak of it — "I fell in love" — makes it sound as if it were some sort of colossal accident, like falling down the stairs. Then later we'll say, "I fell out of love," again as if it weren't within our control. Many people never understand that love really comes from an opening-of-the-heart decision that we can make at any time in our lives.

Yes, love is a choice; it doesn't just happen. But to love, you must first find the happiness within yourself, because when you are unhappy, you are not loving. Once you learn to be happy, you can learn to open your heart to loving. You must also create a place where you refrain from judging those around you, a place of learning, a place where you are present for others at any given moment. Then, when you bring happiness alive in your own life as well as in the lives of others, you are able to love and be loved in return.

I have an unflinchingly optimistic bias. I believe that everyone is lovable — we have only to learn how to see the lovability in others. I also believe that everyone, with absolutely no exceptions, can give love and that one single loving person changes the world.

But how we experience the world and love depends entirely on how we decide to see the world — that is, what we "make up" about the world. I call this "the big make-believe." My wife, Samahria, and I found this truth in our lives when we had a very special child, a child who was autistic and retarded — conditions that all the experts said were incurable and irreversible. They looked at our little boy and said, "Bad, terrible, awful." But we looked at the same child and said, "Wonderful, special, opportunity."

In truth, he wasn't bad, terrible, or awful; nor was he wonderful or an opportunity — these were just things that people "made up" about him. But the important thing is that these beliefs, these perceptions, these labels, led to behaviors. "Bad, terrible, awful" led to distress, despair, and inaction. "Wonderful, special, opportunity" led to optimism, hopefulness, and an incredible amount of creativity and action.

If perceptions lead to behaviors, can our thoughts bring love into our lives? Absolutely. I know for a fact that we can make the choice to love, that we can make that choice come alive, and that it's sustainable, renewable, and ever-deepening. I decided long ago that I wanted to bring love alive, not simply as a mysterious experience beyond my control but as a living principle. And one of the most profound and loving experiences of my life occurred while I was doing just that.

Samahria and I have adopted several children from backgrounds of severe abuse and violence. As we were driving to the airport to pick up one of the children for the first time, I was thinking that the only thing I knew about this little guy was that he was five years old, that when he was two and a half his mom had died, and that his father had tried to kill him by slitting his throat. He had then been put in the back wards of an orphanage. When we were called and asked, "Would you take this little boy, because nobody else will?" we immediately replied, "Absolutely!" because we wanted to open our hearts and our family to him. As we were driving to the airport, I realized that I didn't know this little person but was going to open my arms to him. He would be my son, and I would make a commitment to be his poppy for as long as he wanted me. When we arrived at the airport waiting room and the crowd began to surge through the door, I saw a man I recognized from the orphanage. He was holding the hand of this very frail little five-year-old boy. I dropped down on one knee so I wouldn't seem too large and intimidating and opened my arms to him. I must have been about two hundred feet away, but at some point he saw me, recognized who I was, and started to run toward me. And as I watched my little Robby run toward me, it was as if each step were being taken in slow motion. When he took the first step I thought, "I love you and you are my son." And when he took another step I thought, "And now I love you more and you are my son," and when he took another I thought, "And now I love you even more." By the time he jumped into my arms, I realized that I had accessed the deepest vein of love that I had ever experienced and that I was as passionate about and committed to this little stranger as I was to my other children.

In the definition of love that I gave earlier, I suggested first truly accepting a person and not judging; second, looking into a person's eyes and deeply wanting the best for him or her; and third, taking some sort of positive action to help that person realize his or her potential. I'd like to add the idea of becoming an indiscriminate lover. This kind of indiscriminate loving has nothing to do with sexuality or promiscuity — it's about developing the ability to love anyone and everyone without requiring anything in return. Most of the time we are stingy with our love, thinking, "Well, I'll only love these five people." We do this because we see love as a limited resource. But the most powerful way to develop love is to be indiscriminate, in the sense of not having any requirements for loving. Instead, we immediately open our hearts to the bus driver, the waitress, the flight attendant, and the mail carrier because we want to. And the more we "practice" love this way, the more our lives are filled with love. You can observe the same principle in action when you keep lifting a barbell. Eventually your body responds by increasing the power and size of your biceps. It's a basic tenet of life that the parts of you on which you focus the most attention become the parts that are the most developed. Unfortunately, in our culture we tend to focus an awesome amount of attention on anger, fear, anxiety, judgment, and so on. Just imagine what would happen if we decided to focus on love instead!

One of my kids once said to me, "But, Poppy, if you love everybody, we're not too special to you. You love every stranger on the street, but what about us?" I shared with him that although I might feel I could love a hundred people, a thousand people, or as many people as I could reach out to, each one of those experiences would be special and personal. I didn't mean that when I turned to my son and held out my hand, my love for him would be diminished. It would actually be enhanced, because the more a person focuses on loving, the stronger the ability to love becomes. So I could say that in choosing to love indiscriminately, I make myself a stronger lover and make my ability to love even more powerful.

The focus on love is very important. Some people say, "I want a big car," "I want a better love relationship," or "I want my children to listen to me." Invariably I ask them, "Why do you want those things?" They reply, "Because they'll make me feel good." This mythology implies that when we get what we want, we feel good. But what really happens is that when we get what we think we want, we experience only a temporary feeling of pleasure, inner ease, or peace of mind. The ultimate "feel good" is truly found by filling ourselves with love.

I have discovered that there are certain shortcuts to love and to the happiness that you must have in order to love. First of all, you must learn to be present in each unfolding moment. Instead of living in the past or worrying about the future, make every attempt to concentrate on "right now," because happiness and love are both in the present moment.

Second, make love and happiness priorities in your life. The pursuit of love and happiness often seems to be more tangential than focused. We put a vast amount of time, energy, and money into educating ourselves and pursuing careers, into shopping for furniture, clothes, and vehicles. But we don't expend nearly as much effort to establish a basis for love, happiness, and peace of mind. The decision to put real, focused energy into making love and happiness active states of mind can truly transform your life.

Third, be aware of when you are judging others. Try to let go of those judgments, because they are walls between people. Judgments create hostility, while letting go of them allows you to embrace and love others. If you lead with love, others respond with love.

Next is gratitude — a wonderful precursor to happiness and love. We are often like harried consumers who rush into the store to buy dozens of doughnuts but, once they get home, moan and groan about the holes in the doughnuts. We forget to see the abundance of doughnuts — we see only what's lacking. As you go through your daily activities, allow yourself to look for substance and abundance, rather than focusing on the holes. This attitude goes a long way toward opening your heart, your mind, and your spirit to happy, loving feelings.

And finally, strive for authenticity in both thought and action. One of the great causes of alienation from both ourselves and others is that we avoid presenting who we really are. We often do so for the best of reasons — we don't want to reveal who we are because we're afraid of rejection. But the result is an incredible amount of internal dissonance between the masks and roles we create and our real feelings. By peeling away the masks, dropping the roles, and sharing our true feelings, we can make real connections with our inner selves and with others. That's bridge-building material, bonding material. That's an act of love.

I have an expression that I share with people: we have learned to become beggars of love. Not eaters of love, but beggars. We hold out our cups, asking people to love us — "Will you please love me?" — because we believe that we will feel better if people love us. Unfortunately, the effort is in vain, for we can only really experience love when we fill ourselves with love and when we are willing to pour that love into other people's cups. In order to love others, we must first give ourselves the experience of love inside. At the Option Institute we teach that the one who loves most, wins. That's the heart and soul of the experience of love.

Years ago, when I put myself on the road of the perpetual seeker of love and happiness, I was always searching but didn't have a lot of time. Once I decided that I wanted to change my philosophy from "I seek" to "I find," I realized that in order to "find" I would have to make it a central pursuit in my life. And when I made the pursuit of love and happiness central, I did "find." When I gave this quest the space, the commitment, and the perseverance and reverence, I was able to transform my dream into reality. And by making this an active, central pursuit in your life, you can also bring love and happiness alive for yourself, so that you do not spend your life searching — but finding.

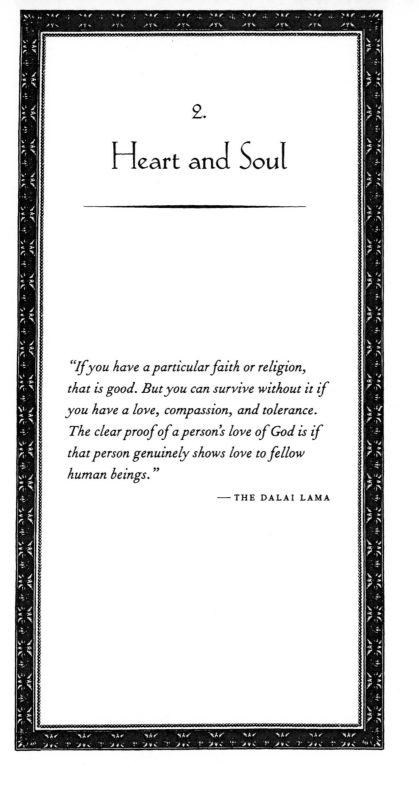

2.

Heart and Soul

"If you have a particular faith or religion, that is good. But you can survive without it if you have a love, compassion, and tolerance. The clear proof of a person's love of God is if that person genuinely shows love to fellow human beings."

— THE DALAI LAMA

TO LOVE AND BE LOVED

BY *Rabbi Harold Kushner*

"None of us has the power to make someone else love us. But we all have the power to give away love, to love other people. And if we do so, we change the kind of person we are, and we change the kind of world we live in."

I WAS IN Oklahoma City a few weeks after the terrible bombing in which so many died, meeting with families who had lost relatives. I asked them, "Of everything that has happened in the last ten weeks, what has helped you most to bear your burden?" And they kept giving me the same answer: the outpouring of support and sympathy from friends and strangers, the validation that they were people worth caring about, that they were right in feeling their pain and grief. The understanding from others made their losses easier to endure.

My wife and I had the same experience in our personal life. Our son died at an early age. When we found out how desperately ill he was, I first had to understand that this wasn't something God was doing to us. We came to understand that God was not punishing us, God was grieving with us. Knowing God was on our side liberated a lot of love and helped us handle the problems better. In the same way, when people reached out to us, it gave us the same message and the same reassurance. People coming forward, just to say that they wanted to help, that they wished there was more they could do, made a difference.

People need to feel understood and supported. Many members of my congregation come to me for counsel. I've learned that they are looking not for advice — often they already know the answer — but for understanding. And I give them my concern, my sense that they are worth caring about and that their problems are worth taking seriously. Receiving this message is immensely therapeutic for them.

I often see how this need simply to be loved with understanding manifests itself in married couples. The wife starts to tell the husband her problems. After a minute he interrupts and tells her what to do about them, because he's geared up to be a problem solver. But she's very unhappy, because she doesn't want his advice. She wants fifteen minutes of his undivided attention. She wants validation that her problems are as important to him as they are to her. And if he would just hold still and listen for those fifteen minutes, she would get the message that he cares about her.

People can do this for one another, can love one another with understanding. All around me I see many people whose lives are not as fulfilling as they might be, simply because these people are too involved with themselves. I think our society puts too much emphasis on finding someone who will love you; our culture focuses too much on being loved and not enough on being a loving person.

It's much easier to be a loving person, to give away love. This ability is something you can have control over. None of us has the power to make someone else love us. But we all have the power to give away love, to love other people. And if we do so, we change the kind of person we are, and we change the kind of world we live in.

This attitude is what works for me in my own marriage. The essence of marital love, I have learned, is not romance, but forgiveness—accepting a person's imperfections and understanding that each of us has his or her quirks that would drive our mates crazy but for the love between us. When I'm in a bad mood, I can only hope that my wife is prepared to write it off as just a bad mood, not the essential me.

Some years ago I read a wonderful newspaper column. A woman sees two children in a playground get into a fight. One of them says, "I hate you. I never want to play with you again." For two or three minutes they play separately, and then they come back and start playing with each other again. The observer says to a woman sitting next to her, "How do children do that? Be so angry one moment and together the next?" And the neighbor says, "Oh, it's easy. They choose happiness over righteousness."

That is the advice I give a lot of married couples. Choose happiness over righteousness. Even if you're right, don't demand recognition of the fact. Sacrifice the victory for the sake of a happy marriage. In a happy marriage there are no winners and losers, only two people who agree to put up with each other—exasperating as that may be.

The rewards are certainly worth it. There is a satisfaction you can find only in a marriage, as you make yourself part of a larger entity. We see this in the biblical injunction that "therefore shall a man leave his father and mother and cleave unto his wife and they shall become one." You achieve a sense of wholeness, not just when you find someone with whom to sleep and live but when you can really join with another person and feel his or her joy, feel his or her pain. There's a sense of expansion of your own self. The emptiness in your life is filled in a way that you can't get from any other human experience.

If you work it right, possessing a sense that there is something greater than you the individual, whether it be spirituality or a child, also creates a sense of happiness and love. I think we all need some sort of force to pull us out of our narcissism and our overconcern for ourselves. Having a child can do this. I've seen how a child changes people, just knowing that this other life is dependent on them. A sense of religious commitment can do this, too. It opens the heart, bringing a sense that you owe something to a cause greater than your own well-being or your own satis-factions. I think human beings are created to be this way, and when we act selfishly and narcissistically, we're acting against our essential nature. People are not meant to be selfish.

People are meant to be loving, and they are meant to be intermittently happy. I suspect that people who are happy all the time probably don't realize what's going on around them. There is so much pain in the world, only by shutting our eyes to it could we always be happy. But we do have the power to always be loving, always be caring. And from time to time, we have a moment of happiness that justifies everything that leads up to it.

This runs counter to a lot of the messages all around us: that if we just get a certain something — a better car, a better neighborhood, a better pair of sneakers — then we'll be happy. Of course, this frame of mind doesn't work. It only makes us more insecure. Advertisers need to make us feel anxious so that we'll buy whatever they're selling to make us feel better. And insecurity makes it hard for us to feel worthy of love, to believe that others will accept us if they really know us, and ultimately to be accepting of other people.

Someone once wrote: "Happiness is always a by-product. You don't make yourself happy by chasing happiness. You make yourself happy by being a good person." The happiest people I know are people who don't even think about being happy. They just think about being good neighbors, good people. And then happiness sort of sneaks in the back window while they're busy doing good.

This attitude works in relationships as well. I always worry about a relationship in which one or both parties are constantly taking the temperature of the relationship and measuring whether they're happy. I suspect that such an appraisal leads to asking questions like, "Would I be happier if I were in a relationship with somebody else?" Instead of asking themselves, "Am I happy?" I think they should ask themselves, "Is there something I can do to make this a better relationship? What else can I give to it?" If they do that enough, they'll turn around one day and realize happiness has snuck up on them.

Being loving toward others, and creating a relationship in which they love us, is a reciprocal process. We begin by being loving toward ourselves, seeing ourselves as capable of loving, capable of giving things away. It's a very stunted person who can't give him- or herself away emotionally because of being afraid there won't be much left if he or she does. Loving ourselves doesn't mean narcissism and self-worship. It means accepting the imperfections in ourselves and realizing that nobody expects us to be perfect. Self-love means seeing that not every mistake is a permanent stain on our self-esteem and our sense of worthiness. That's how you love yourself. I worry about people whose major goal in life is getting enough love, because I think they end up being takers rather than givers.

It helps to have some moral code in achieving these things. We act against our essential nature when we are dishonest or devious or selfish. And acting against our essential nature impinges on our ability to give and receive love and on our ability to experience happiness. For example, adultery corrodes a marriage because it introduces an element of dishonesty.

I have trouble understanding people who do things that, in the long run, are only going to hurt them. This self-damage could be in the way they eat and drink or behave with their families. Probably what is happening is that they're not confident that they'll get enough love, so they go out and steal it, just as people who feel they don't have enough money rob people. People who are worried that they're not going to get enough love try to get love by unethical means. This isn't just limited to marital infidelity. For example, a woman trying to get love by illicit means might pretend to be someone she isn't. She wears a mask when she's suppressing her own individuality, her own needs and wants. She's hoping to be loved by people who wouldn't love her if they knew what she was really like.

I don't think people who do this realize how inherently contradictory it is. How can it be real, nourishing love when it's gained dishonestly? When they are hiding their true nature? It is always a futile pursuit, it always catches up with them. And ironically, they stay hungry.

I think in the long run we love people who, by accepting us, enable us to be better than we otherwise would be. We love someone who reflects to us an image of ourselves that makes us feel good about ourselves. We love someone who frees up the creative and emotional energies that otherwise would remain dormant. We love someone, too, who helps us to be a loving person.

Some religions, like some people, have the kind of message that liberates our own ability to love. If the message of the religion is "God loves you despite your shortcomings," your heart is opened to giving and receiving love. But if the message we hear is "You have sinned, you have fallen short, you're no good, God is disappointed in you," we're going to tighten up. It turns us into emotional misers, unable to give away love. But if the message is "God knows exactly who you are, and loves you anyway," we are permitted to love and to forgive — ourselves and the other imperfect people in our lives.

There are a lot of religious spokespeople who don't agree with me, but I believe that God really did make us in his own image — a model of love and forgiveness that we can emulate. This is very important. This is how I try to live my life.

I recognize that I need love in the same way that I need food and sleep and exercise. I understand that my soul would shrivel up from malnutrition if I didn't love, didn't give love and receive love. One of the things that works for me, helps me fill my heart with love, is the series of Jewish prayers that focus on being grateful for all the things around us that we might otherwise take for granted. The first words of prayer when Jews wake up in the morning are to thank God that they're still alive and awake, that their bodies work, their arms, their legs, their eyes, their minds work, that they have clothes to wear and food to eat and things to look forward to. When your heart is filled with gratitude, when you can just go out and feel how lucky you are that the world is there for you, and how lucky you are that there are people out there trying to enrich your world, it's a lot easier to be loving — to yourself and to others.

HEARTWORK

BY *Marianne Williamson*

"That's what we're talking about here: whether the spirit of love is in charge of our thought forms. And if it is, we're more charitable; we give people a break. We bless instead of condemn. We support instead of deride. We forgive instead of attack. We love instead of fear."

PEOPLE DON'T NEED to be reminded of love's importance. What people are looking for are the what and how of love. The culture in which we have grown up is dominated by a severely loveless mentality, and fully recognizing this is crucial to our healing as a nation. Without that conscious recognition, we fail to understand what difficult work it is internally, as well as externally, to avoid complicity with loveless cultural stimuli and to resist effectively their persuasiveness.

The great teachings of the ages apply as much to the experience of this culture at this time as they do to any culture at any other time. The heart lives in an eternal realm.

The only way we can reach that realm is to bypass the ca-cophony of the world, to reach deep into our own hearts for the silence that waits for each of us.

If we wake up in the morning and head directly into the turmoil of the world — reading the headlines, watching or listening to the news as the status quo defines it — then the mind has no opportunity to escape the world's hysteria. But if we meditate and pray before we see the headlines, or at least before we head off into our worldly activities, then our hope and faith remain firm.

I think we're on the earth to bring healing to the world, but we can hardly do so when we ourselves are too wounded. We are all heir to the fear that runs rampant in this culture. When we do not turn toward God, we be-come expressions of the hysteria. Behavior modification or mere suppression of the panic is not enough to trans-mute our minds or the conditions around us. Only love can do that.

The world's greatest need, I believe, is for serious spiri-tual practice. Pascal wrote: "All of humanity's problems stem from man's inability to sit quietly in a room alone."

In the *Course of Miracles,* it says that five minutes spent with the Holy Spirit in the morning is enough to guar-antee that He will be in charge of our thought forms throughout the day. That's what we're talking about here: whether the spirit of love is in charge of our thought forms. And if it is, we're more charitable; we give people a break. We bless instead of condemn. We support instead of deride. We forgive instead of attack. We love instead of fear.

We are all heir to the darkness of this world, and we are all heir to the gifts of God. To choose His gifts over the false gifts of the world is a moment-by-moment choice, a moment-by-moment decision. But we live in a world where the stimulus of fear is so loud, so insidious, and so constantly bombarding us that the work of resistance is serious work indeed.

It's a kind of muscle training. If you want a new body, you have to work for it; if you want a new mind, you have to work for it also. Spiritual practice takes a very deep effort, to soften our own hearts, to quiet our own fears, to renew our own souls. It all begins within us, and the work can be grueling.

My most difficult spiritual challenge of the past few years has been my relationship with my daughter. I never knew how hard parenting would be. I don't mean physically, but emotionally. Whatever intimacy issues that I have are magnified in my relationship with her.

I have had to work to become someone who can read to her for an hour without jumping up to answer the phone. I have had to work to get myself to take her to school and pick her up, myself, consistently, rather than always choosing to put work first. These might sound like small things, but to me they were big things. Work, particularly its adrenaline-driven dimensions, has become an American addiction — and it's a killer. It doesn't let you rest. A driven woman is not much of a mother, so I have worked very hard to reclaim my quiet. Things are better now, but I realize the level of sustained effort it takes to be the mother I want to be. I know in my heart that I can write books or give lectures to lots of people, and that's great, but being a good parent is much more important than any other job.

As Gandhi said, "We must *be* the change."

THE WELLSPRING OF
THE HEART

BY *Jack Kornfield*

"The questions asked at the end of his or her life are very simple ones: 'Did I love well? Did I love the people around me, my community, the earth, in a deep way?'"

I F YOU WANT to love, take the time to listen to your heart. In most ancient and wise cultures, it is a regular practice for people to talk to their heart. There are rituals, stories, and meditative skills in every spiritual tradition that awaken the voice of the heart. To live wisely, this practice is essential, because our heart is the source of our connection to and intimacy with all of life. And life *is* love. This mysterious quality of love is all around us, as real as gravity.

Yet how often we forget about love! Love begins by recognizing what most deeply fulfills us is not what we have or what we do, but the state of our heart. The Indian mystic poet Kabir wrote: "Are you looking for Me? I am in the next seat. My shoulder is against yours." Here he speaks of our longing for the Beloved.

Our heart is very near, yet in modern life a remarkable swoon comes over us in the complexity and busyness of our time, and we forget what matters most. We think we have time, but no one knows for sure how much time he or she really has. In his teachings to Carlos Castaneda, Don Juan uses death as an advisor to remind us of these values:

> Death is our eternal companion. It is always to our left at an arm's length. It has always been watching us, and it always will until the day it taps us. The thing to do when you're impatient with your life, turn to your left and ask advice from your death. An immense amount of pettiness is dropped if your death makes a gesture to you, or if you catch a glimpse of it, or if you just catch the feeling that your companion is there watching you.

If you have the privilege of being at the bedside of someone having a conscious death, the questions asked at the end of his or her life are very simple ones: "Did I love well? Did I love the people around me, my community, the earth, in a deep way?" And perhaps, "Did I live fully? Did I offer myself to life?"

In the heart of each of us, there is a voice of knowing, a song that can remind us of what we most value and long for, what we have known since we were a child. There is a tribe in East Africa that recognizes this song even before birth. In this tribe the birth date of a child is not considered the day of his or her physical birth or even the day of conception, as in other village cultures. For this tribe the birth date is the first time the child is a thought in his or her mother's mind. Aware of her intention to conceive a child with a particular man, the mother goes off to sit alone under a great tree. There she sits and listens deeply, until she can hear the song of the child she hopes will be born. Once she has heard this song, she returns to her village and teaches it to the father, so they can sing it together as they make love, inviting the child to join them. After the child is conceived, she sings the song to the baby in her womb. She then teaches it to the old women and midwives of the village, so that throughout the labor and at the miraculous moment of birth itself, the child is greeted with its song. After the birth all the villagers learn the song of their new member and sing it to the child when he or she falls or hurts him- or herself. It is sung in times of triumph or in rituals and initiations. When the child grows up, this song becomes a part of his or her marriage ceremony; and at the end of life, his or her loved ones gather around the deathbed and sing the song for the last time.

Hearing such a story brings a yearning for such listening, for our own lives and song to be held and guided from such a place of respect. But we have been distracted and drawn into the marketplace. Our lives are complex, and our times are materialistic, ambitious, outer-directed. So often we have forgotten how to listen. It is difficult to be in touch with our heart in the midst of a busy life.

Anne Wilson Schaef, who writes about the addicted society, tells us that

> the best adjusted person in modern society is the person who is not dead and not alive, just numb, a zombie. When you're dead, you're not able to contribute work to the society, and when you're fully alive you must constantly say no to many of the processes of society — the racism, the polluted environment, the nuclear threat, the arms race, drinking unsafe water, and eating carcinogenic foods. Thus, it is in the interest of

modern consumer society to promote those things that take the edge off and keep us busy with our fixes, or keep us slightly numbed out and zombie-like. In this way, our modern consumer society functions as an addict.

No wonder we have difficulty staying in touch with our heart! When we do speak with our heart, we must ask the most honest questions we can. How do we feel about the way we are living? Is it conducive to ease, creativity, wholeness, respect? Or have the responsibilities of our adult life made a prison for our body and spirit?

For many of us, our loss of innocence and connection began years ago in childhood, when they became buried to allow us to survive our schools, families, religion, and culture. And so part of the art of living from the heart is reclaiming this childlike capacity to listen to our heart. The famous American painter James McNeill Whistler attended West Point Military Academy in the 1850s. In his engineering class, the instructor asked all students to draw a model of a bridge. Whistler drew a beautiful stone arched bridge, complete with two young boys fishing from it. The lieutenant, very angry, said, "This is a military exercise. Get those children off the bridge." So Whistler redrew it and put the boys fishing from the bank of the river. The lieutenant got even angrier and said, "I told you to get them completely out of the picture." So in the last version, Whistler drew the stone bridge and the river, and added two little tombstones on the riverside with children's names on them! This is a symbol of the way that many of us have lost our heart and, ultimately, lost connection with ourselves. In fact, it took Whistler many years of painting to reawaken the spirit of the child in himself. Like Whistler, most of us must find our own way to reclaim our buried tears and grief and, passing through them, rediscover a renewed source of playfulness and joy.

The great traditions of meditation and prayer, of contemplative life, offer ways that help us to listen deeply, to restore this lost connection. One of the qualities they foster that allows us to stay in touch with our heart is stillness. We need to step out of "doing" time, to "being." We need a Sabbath, a regular holy day, a regular time to stop and reconnect with the spirit that moves through all things. Even doing too many good deeds can be a problem for us. As Thomas Merton said, "To allow oneself to be carried away by a multitude of conflicting concerns, to surrender to too many demands, to commit oneself to too many good projects, to want to help everyone and everything, is itself to succumb to the violence of our time."

So what we seek in living from the heart is a rhythm in life that includes time for renewal in nature: time to walk for no purpose at all; time to sit still; time to listen to the sounds of life around us; time to listen to our bodies; time to listen to our hearts. Meditation can teach us this art with the simple grace of following our breath in and out until we feel the life rhythm that always moves in our bodies. Then we can listen to the stories the mind is telling, to the longings of the heart, and to the things we most deeply value. Meditation cultivates a quality of sacred attention. It is a prayer that doesn't ask for what we want, but opens us to hear, "Not my will but Thine": a prayer that listens with the whole being.

This kind of respect of self, in stillness, in nature, in prayer, can naturally extend to touch the hearts of others. When we listen to another, we can meet him or her with an agenda or with openness. We can try to get our point across, defend ourselves, accomplish just what we want, or protect ourselves. All this comes from what in the spiritual world is called "the body of fear." Or we can listen with sacred attention, with respect, in order to learn what is true in the heart of this other being.

This love, this connection of the heart, this intimacy, is not far away. As Mother Teresa says, "In this world, we cannot do great things. We can only do small things with great love." It's not very complicated to do these small things. When we become still, the path is obvious. It is made of the moments and the days of being there for ourselves and our children, listening to our colleagues, and honoring the environment. When we are present with our heart, we offer a respect to ourselves and to others in any situation.

Even in our modern technological world, a renewal of this respect is possible. For example, a series of medical facilities based on a patient-centered model called Plaintree Hospitals are opening up. Classical music plays softly in the background. Patients wear their own robes and pajamas, sleep on flowered sheets, and are encouraged to sleep as late as they like in the morning. Friends and family are welcome to visit at any time convenient for the patient. They are encouraged to help and cook and care for the patient. The idea makes so much sense. And this is true of ways of the heart as well. What we most care for, what we most need to do, is right there — when we take the time to listen.

Sometimes, however, we become afraid. We don't recognize that the heart has the capacity to be open in the midst of all things. I have a friend, a businessman, who began to meditate. He began to have so much chest pain that he thought he was having a heart attack. We worked together and he breathed gently into the pain, putting his hand on his heart. When he let himself feel the busyness that had run his life for such a long time, tears welled up for the things he'd left undone in his family and his community. The pains of his heart subsided. And he realized that he could live in a very different way.

Often when we first try to listen to the heart, there is sorrow. The unfinished business we've run from, the grief not felt, the losses that are part of our measure of sorrow, the tears of the world, make themselves known. We can open to them, too, and listen in a sacred or respectful way; we can allow the greatness of our heart to unfold. A woman I know tells the story of how each morning on her way to work she passed a homeless man; for months she dropped coins into his cup and gradually developed a nodding relationship with him. Then one day she realized that she had never looked him in the eye. She felt that if she ever truly did so, he'd end up in her living room the next week. She realized that she had closed down.

Like this woman, we are all afraid that we cannot hold the sorrow and beauty of the world. And it is true that the heart has its seasons, just as a flower opens to the sunlight and closes to the night. We need to be respectful of those rhythms. But we can't close down for long. It is our true nature to have an open heart, as much as it is the true nature of a flower to open in the sunlight. Sometimes this is called our Buddha nature, or our divine nature. But whatever we call it, know that each heart has an enormous capacity to hold the world. We are intimately connected with all things, and whether we let ourselves know it or not, our heart feels all that is true in life. Mahatma Gandhi used to say it this way: "I believe in the essential unity of all that lives. Therefore, I believe that if one person gains spiritually, the whole world gains, and that if one person falls, the whole world falls to that extent."

This is not just a philosophy. My wife and I were traveling in India some years ago; we were visiting a mountain-top temple of a great sage, a woman named Vimala Thakar. My wife began to have very painful visions of the death of her brother, which I thought were just part of her meditation process. But quite sadly, one week later we received a telegram that read "Your brother has died, a suicide." The way he had died was exactly what my wife had seen in her vision — and we learned from the telegram that her vision had come on the very night of her brother's death. Here we were, halfway around the earth, and yet my wife knew very well what had happened to her brother and how it had happened. We have all heard such stories. This is because in reality we *are* all connected.

So the work of our heart, the work of taking time, to listen, to live our values, to love well, is also our gift to the whole of the world. Through our inner courage, we awaken to the greatest capacity of human life, the one true human freedom: to love in the midst of all things. Viktor Frankl, the famous psychiatrist who lived through the Holocaust, wrote:

> We who lived in the concentration camps can remember those who walked through the huts comforting others, giving away their last piece of bread. They may have been few in number, but they offer sufficient proof that everything can be taken from a human being but one thing — the last of our freedoms — to choose our spirit in any given set of circumstances.

The power of the heart is enormous and transformative. Each of us has our own gifts that come from the flowering of our heart. It may be to plant a garden; run an ethical business; be a teacher or a healer, an artist or a parent. For some the journey to the heart's generosity is long and hard; but even those who are abused as children can grow out of those difficult circumstances to be beautiful adults in our community. I have seen it in my work again and again. Always those wounded adults remember one person — a teacher, a grandparent, a friend — who saw them or touched them or loved them, even in the midst of grave abuse and torment. And it is on this love that they base their healing.

The strength of the heart is its ability to nurture all that is beautiful in human life. It requires from us a great mercy and forgiveness — not judgment but the tenderness that weeps at the sorrow of another as if it were our own and that is willing to offer quick forgiveness. By forgiveness, I do not mean condoning what causes suffering to us or to others. Forgiveness, in the end, is simply the statement that we shall not put another human being out of our heart. That we are willing to let go of the pain of the past so that we can start again on the basis of love. There is a story of two ex–prisoners of war who met many years later. One asked the other, "Have you forgiven your captors yet?" And the second man said, "No, never!" And the first one said, "Well, then, they still have you in prison, don't they?"

So the work of the heart is simply the work of mercy for ourselves and for others. It is as natural to us as our own breath. It is who we are. As Thomas Merton wrote:

Then it was as if I suddenly saw the secret beauty of their hearts, the depths of their hearts where neither sin nor knowledge can reach the core of their reality, the person that each one is in God's eyes. If only they could see themselves as they really are. If only we could see each other that way, there would be no more need for war or hatred, no more need for cruelty or greed. I suppose the big problem would be that we would fall down and worship each other.

This is the work of the heart. It comes from the intention to listen, to take time to feel your breath, to sense your heart beating in your body, to look at the movement of the clouds and the change of the season. Ask your heart, "If my life were only a little bit longer, what is most important, what do I value, how do I want to live?" As we practice listening to the heart and bringing it forth in our actions, in our tongue, we discover that love itself changes our universe. It is contagious — we catch it from one another. And the power of loving-kindness, the power of those living from the heart, makes the power of armies and technology seem like child's play. For it is the heart force that brings all life, that creates all life, that moves through us. It is never too late to touch this fountain. So take time to listen, to allow that wellspring to be known in your own life.

THE BASICS OF LOVE

BY *Betty Eadie*

"The more you notice the love, the miracles, and the beauty around you, the more love comes into your life. The more you love, the greater your ability to love. And the process perpetuates itself. As you love the world and the people in it, you find this love manifests itself and returns to you."

FILLING YOUR LIFE with love — both giving and receiving — is one of the most difficult aspects of life to master. At least it was for me, for mine was not always a lovable world. Nor are all people loving or easy to love. To make matters worse, many of us have been raised in families that have taught us the opposite — to be nonloving.

I had to learn not only how to give love but also how to receive it. It is often easier to act in a loving manner than to acknowledge the love of others or to trust in the love of others.

I learned to fill my life with love by first learning to love myself. I found that when I wasn't acting in loving ways to others, it was invariably because something unacceptable was going on inside me. At those times, it seemed that most of the people in my life were bothering and annoying me. Fortunately, I discovered that this bother was stemming from something missing within me, from a lack of self-esteem — self-love — and it usually had nothing to do with "them." I knew that to fully love others, first I had to feel love for myself.

It's easy to find fault in others, but much more difficult to look at ourselves and our own faults with honesty. We're often in denial about our own faults; we don't like to see them too clearly. After taking a look at my own flaws — some of which I could change, others of which I simply had to accept — I was gradually able to recognize my faults as parts of me that needed ongoing work. Rather than insisting that I was perfect and that everyone else was to blame, I was able to begin loving and accepting myself as never before. And, having learned to accept and love myself, I was able to extend love and acceptance to others. I was free to start loving the less than perfect parts of other people as well.

Of course, my near-death experience affected my outlook on life, filling me with a desire to become a more loving individual. (I would like to think that I would have become more loving anyway. Time and age have a way of encouraging this!) At this point in my life I don't focus on the many reasons why I wanted to become more loving. Instead, I try to focus and act on the many possibilities for being a loving person that arise each day. Often a simple desire to change is all you really need to begin.

One of the ways I practice love is to think about how I would feel in a given circumstance if the roles were reversed. How would I want someone to respond to me? I then try to act accordingly. And you know, it really works. When we make a genuine attempt to treat others as we would like to be treated, we become much kinder, more compassionate, and more tolerant. No one wants to be hurt or to be treated unkindly or disrespectfully. And although many of us were taught to treat others as we would like to be treated, we usually insist that others extend this courtesy to *us* before we do so. We have to reverse this process. If we were the ones to offer love and kindness, even if we didn't always get something in return, we would live in a much more loving world.

It's important to love and appreciate the little things in life, all the beauty that God has created. I know it sounds terribly simplistic, but as I go about my day, I try to appreciate *everything* I see: a bird, a tree, a flower, something unusual happening. My goal is to love what I see and to thank God for showing it to me. When I do, it's as though the universe opens up and envelops me in love. As I receive this love, I can't help become increasingly open and available for more. A wonderful expanding cycle begins to take place. The more you notice the love, the miracles, and the beauty around you, the more love comes into your life. The more you love, the greater your ability to love. And the process perpetuates itself. As you love the world and the people in it, you find this love manifests itself and returns to you.

As you focus on being a more loving person — without worrying about what you are getting in return — you find that plenty of love *does* flow into your life. You don't have to do anything, it just happens. People who are loving and giving attract kindred souls into their lives, for it is easy to love those who are themselves loving. You attract loving people and acts of kindness into your life as you yourself become more loving. It's a giant circle of love that begins with you.

When you act in a loving fashion, an important ripple effect takes place. And even in those rare instances when your love for someone is not returned, it's a good idea simply to keep loving. This doesn't mean that you should allow yourself to be taken advantage of, but rather that you become a model of love and loving behavior. You may be able to help lead that person to another level, where he or she might be kinder somewhere down the road.

We often think the big things are what really matter, but that's not always true. Never underestimate the importance of loving acts. One tiny kind deed can make a world of difference — and you may never even know it. You can probably remember, somewhere back in your life, something that someone said or did that made a big difference to you. This person may have said one simple little thing that stuck with you forever. I remember being in a hospital when I was a little girl, probably when I was around twelve years old. A nurse came into the room and when I opened my eyes, she said to another nurse, "Such love and kindness come out of this little girl's eyes." That comment has stuck with me to this day. It has helped me to think of myself as a kind, loving person. I look upon the nurse's comment as an affirmation of love. To this day, I like to share my love through my eyes. (Eyes are, of course, "the window to the soul.") I'm sure that this wonderful nurse would never remember saying her kind words, nor could she imagine the impact her kindness has had on my life. In a sense, then, she has indirectly helped everyone that I have helped.

The wisest words about love come from the Bible: Do unto others as you would have them do unto you. I have found this to be good advice — always stop and think before you respond or act out of unkindness or harshness. Imagine how you would feel, and how you would like to be treated, if you were in that person's shoes. The true blessing of offering love comes when you don't need to do something for someone, but you do it anyway — for no other reason than your desire to be loving. In these instances, you, as well as the person you are loving, are truly blessed.

LOVE ENOUGH FOR ALL

BY *Stephen R. Covey, Ph.D.*

"Individuals can affect the world by becoming a model or an example in their small circle of influence. Just as a rock thrown into a pond causes ripples to gradually keep going out until eventually they are very small, so our acts influence the ecology of the entire human race."

I LOOK UPON LOVE as the supreme activity of life. Developing love in yourself has to take priority. You need to draw upon the divine energy from God so that you have the power to manifest or express this kind of love. Then the word *love* is no longer a noun. This word *love* becomes a verb. It's something that you do, a sacrifice you make.

A couple came to me to talk about the unhappiness in their marriage. The husband said, "What do you suggest I do, because the feeling isn't in our marriage anymore?" I said, "Well then, *just love her.*" He said, "Well, Stephen, the problem is that the feeling isn't there. It really isn't, not on my part, not on her part; but we are still concerned because we have children." I said, "Where did you get this concept that love is a feeling? Love is a verb; love is something you do. Look at any mother who goes to the Valley of the Shadow of Death to bring a child into the world. The love she has for that child didn't come from the child, it came from her, because she sacrificed for the child. Love — the feeling — is the result, the fruit, of love. The concept of love as a feeling comes from Hollywood. It's selfish and immature, not holy and divine."

This was an exciting new thought for the husband. If love is truly a verb, if forgiveness is a verb, if kindness is a verb, then you can do something about it. But if love is just a feeling, you feel almost helpless because you think you have no control over your feelings. Ultimately, your feelings are a function of your actions. Since you have control over your actions, you therefore have control over your feelings. As you gradually discover this, you gain the maturity to love — whether you are loved in return or not.

The key to love means having a source of unconditional love that you can draw upon endlessly. To me, the way God loves his children is a kind of "fatherly" love that is a rich, unconditional love. "Brotherly" love, which is more conditional, is great; but when push comes to shove in life, brotherly love tends to break down into personal differences. It is during these times that people need to embrace the divine fatherly love.

When you love God first, you love your spouse more. When you love God first, you love your children more. You should always love God first, not people first. Then you have the power to love people with rich and unconditional fatherly love. You may even have to be strong and strict with people sometimes, but that's what a father does with a son or daughter. You transcend the personal when you love God; yet in doing so, you feed the heart and soul of both you and the other person.

To tap into this source of boundless love takes spiritual effort; but when it comes, it is like being nourished by a spring. If I neglect that spring, that source of nourishment, for only a few days or sometimes for even a few hours — if the stresses of life are great enough — then my ability to love unconditionally is no longer there.

I find that just as you have a one-on-one relationship with God, you must have a one-on-one relationship with all the key people in your life and teach them to have a similar relationship with the key people in their lives, so that the water of this love "goes to the end of the row," as the farmer might say. It's important to have private visits with every key person in your life on a regular basis. I try to do so with my married children at least monthly, the un-married ones at least weekly, and with my wife and children at home daily.

I believe the true test of any family is how the parents treat the child who challenges them the most. If you can show unconditional love toward that one child, then all the other children know that the love expressed toward them is also unconditional. But if you cannot show that uncon-ditional love to the one who tries your patience, who may even repel you emotionally, the moment you don't affirm their value, all the other children question the love that you give to them. They wonder, Well, if I hit your nerve, will I also be withdrawn from this affection?

I remember one time when I was with my little boy and I was being unkind and critical of someone. My surprised son turned to me and asked, "Dad, do you love me?" He meant, "Do I have to worry that if I do something wrong, your love will be withdrawn just as it was toward that person?" Assuring him that I loved him unconditionally, I owned up to my mistake and said that only God is perfect and that I, too, needed to work on my own mind and heart.

A powerful source of the ability to love intrinsically is to give service anonymously, when no one knows the source, not even the recipient. If the recipient does know, there should be no effort to get any mileage or recognition out of it. You should not even tell your own heart that you know. A powerful affirmation comes inside your soul when you give anonymous service in this way. When your service is seen, you can transfer all the credit and the glory to God, who gave you the gift and the resources to do it.

When acting unconditionally, you learn not to take either credit or criticism personally. You have to be impervious to how people treat you, to maintain your own sense of personal worth and security. Your behavior has to come from your integrity and a deeply imbedded set of principles and values that ultimately are centered upon God.

Love in the workplace is the cement that enables all the connections to flow smoothly. Without it, the workplace is a machine without lubricant. Love in the workplace manifests itself in many ways: empathy, respect, courtesies, kindness, keeping promises to other people, never talking behind another's back in a negative way. If you have concerns or criticisms, go directly to the person and share them with an "I" message rather than a "you" message. When you have concerns, you say, "My perception is" or "My feeling is," which is a softer form of giving feedback. It's important to care enough to give feedback to everyone — customers, suppliers, and all your associates inside the company.

The word *love* may be too saccharine for some people in the business context; if so, *caring* will suffice. Sincerity, sacrifice, service, respect, dignity, fairness, and patience are manifestations of love and caring. It doesn't matter what words are used, because the focus is on building good relationships. Relationships in selling, relationships in consulting — they're all about love.

Love makes the world go around, no question about it. The absence of it makes people defensive so that they are not vulnerable. Most people don't know how to tap into the unconditional supply of love, so if they see only conditional sources being taken away, they become cynical and develop different reactions, which psychologists call projection, rationalization, intellectualization, denial, and so forth. When people put on the armor of God that Saint Paul talked about, they have spirit and the word with them and have no need to defend themselves with sarcasm or cynicism.

Self-control and self-esteem are necessary to forget yourself. Then you become capable of really living outside yourself with love. Otherwise, you become narcissistic and see the world through your own very narrow frame. You live love on your terms but don't include a frame of reference for other people. You begin to make deposits into their emotional bank account, but these deposits may not truly reflect the unique realities or needs of those people at all. What you perceive as deposits may actually be very low-level deposits or even possible withdrawals.

We also affect the world by being prayerful. Prayer taps into the energy of God, bringing the heavenly forces on the other side to bear on this side. When someone prays in faith for someone, although he or she may not be connected in time or space (perhaps that person is on a different continent, or perhaps that person is in prison), I don't know how it happens, but the energy of God touches that person in the form of protection or perhaps a sense of peace and comfort. Fundamentally, I believe the kindest thing we can ever do for other people is to give them love and prayer. They may not ever know we are doing it.

Individuals can affect the world by becoming a model or an example in their small circle of influence. Just as a rock thrown into a pond causes ripples to gradually keep going out until eventually they are very small, so our acts influence the ecology of the entire human race. The poet Robert Browning once said, "One man's death diminishes me no matter where it is." We are all part of one another and so, interwoven; it's a kind of divine architectural ecology that encompasses us all and cannot be violated.

3.

Giving and Receiving

---

*"Love cures people — both the ones who
give it and the ones who receive it."*

—DR. KARL MENNINGER (1893–1990)

THE BIRTHRIGHT OF
OUR HEART

BY *Benjamin Shield, Ph.D.*

"This is the essence that gives breath to our bodies and to our souls. This is the breath of God. It infuses each of us with life and purpose. It endows us with the grace to give and receive the way our bodies breathe out and breathe in."

LOVE IS THERE — always. Yet it is often difficult to fully embrace this wellspring of love that resides within ourselves and is available to us each and every moment. It is not something that we must create, it *is* us. Love is our essence — the fundamental energy that nourishes us. It is our birthright.

From our creation we are sent on a journey to reclaim our birthright. When we encounter obstacles along the way, we continue the journey — not by overpowering something *outside* ourselves, but by letting go of something *inside* ourselves. We do this by keeping our hearts open, risking vulnerability, letting go of past hurtful experiences that block our ability to love, and allowing others to love us.

We could say that love is like the sun. Clouds may pass over it and temporarily block its warmth. But the sun, like our essence, continues to shine. Our lives may move between joy and disappointment, but the love within us never diminishes. We can ignore, hinder, and even deny this love — but we cannot destroy it. We can forget love, but love does not forget us.

Love creates the strong foundation for our lives. And it is often the simplest of loving moments that continue to strengthen this foundation. I am often reminded of a story that I heard some time ago. A radio commentator was talking about her vacation at a beautiful seaside town in Mexico. One afternoon she saw an elderly couple strolling hand in hand along the beach. They were clearly in love, and there was something about them that made the commentator feel that they had been married forever.

Later that day she saw this same couple at dinner. Her curiosity got the better of her, and she apologetically introduced herself and asked the secret of their wonderful relationship. The answer surprised her.

The woman was genuinely amused. "Our secret is that my husband has always been a bit hard of hearing! You see, we were married during the Depression. Both of us worked two, sometimes three, jobs just to make ends meet. One day I came home so exhausted, I said to my husband, 'I'm so tired, my *teeth* hurt!' Well, he took me by the hand, sat me down, took off my shoes, and lovingly rubbed my *feet!*"

She continued, "I think you understand the mix-up! But from that day on, this became our little ritual. At the end of each day, my husband has always lovingly rubbed my feet. With this simple act, he shows me daily how much he loves me and, in turn, I remember how much I love him. And no matter what else is going on in our lives, or in the world, we always remember how easy it is to love each other."

There are many times that I find myself afraid to take the risk of loving, to become vulnerable and tenderly open-hearted with another human being. The wounds from hurtful experiences have created fears and obstacles that hinder my ability to love. Learning to identify and remove those fears is one of life's most challenging processes. When I feel overwhelmed and afraid to love, I try to remind myself that love, not fear, is the template upon which our world is built.

Much of my inner work involves releasing the fears — past, present, and future — that interfere with my access to love and love's access to me. This is a lifelong process of facing myself consciously, discovering that my fears are just masks for old pain and not premonitions about the future. In this process of letting go, I try to focus on those things in my life that nourish the experience of love. I try to focus on those things that help me to let my ego boundaries melt, to lose my self-importance, and to release my daily worries.

We do not have to sequester ourselves in a monastery to do this. The unique, daily moments that each of us have in our lives can continually reconnect us with love. Watching my dog, Annie, play with her friends, I feel the unabashed joy she experiences. Listening to music such as Beethoven's "Moonlight Sonata" wash over me and infuse me with its beauty softens the harsh edges of the day. Simple acts, such as taking a walk in the woods, holding a door open for a stranger, or just remembering to breathe deeply and consciously are all things that help me to give up some of my limitations, to let myself expand, become more spacious, and to move myself gently toward that center of my being, into the heart of love.

This ongoing process of connecting with my center enables me to merge more fully with others. When this occurs, my perspective widens, my senses sharpen, and I become more permeable to the love within me and to the love given by those around me.

Love is more than thought and feeling. Love is behavior. It means spending time with our children as they struggle bravely to read. It means being with friends as we allow them the space and opportunity to share their lives, their dreams, and sometimes their tears. It means really trying to see things through another's eyes. We become renewed by giving our love away — in our relationships, our work, our communities, and most important, to ourselves.

Equally important is the action of letting love *in*. We do harm to ourselves and to those around us when we withhold the events of our day, when we brush off a compliment, or when we refuse to let our mates hold and comfort us. We not only starve our own heart, but at the same time deprive our partners' heart of the joy of giving.

Sometimes love is not found in the "doing." It is often discovered in the quiet moments, in the nurturing of ourselves or others, in the space we create in our lives for love to enter.

The folly of chasing after love is reflected in the story of the Zen student searching for enlightenment. He was so overzealous that he spent morning, noon, and night meditating and praying, and seldom stopped to eat or sleep. His Zen teacher worried as he watched his student become weaker and more exhausted each day. Eventually, he sat down with him and expressed his concern.

"Why do you not eat and get the rest that your body and spirit deserve?" he asked.

"Because I seek enlightenment and there is not a moment to waste."

The teacher placed his hand on the student's shoulder and replied, "What makes you rush ahead after enlightenment? Perhaps all your hurrying carries you *away* from what you seek. Maybe enlightenment is actually behind you, and all you need to do is stand still and let it catch up with you!"

This story reminds me that we can choose to judge ourselves, or to love ourselves. When we are in judgment, we become carried away by the failures and heartbreaks of the past or transported forward into the idealistic fantasies of the future. We hurry backward and forward, desperately seeking the love that already rests patiently inside our own hearts, waiting to be discovered. In the moments that we consciously transcend judgment, self-criticism, and self-doubt, we create the environment for compassion and love for ourselves as well as others.

The effects of experiencing genuine compassion reach far beyond our own lives. It can transform our world in ways we could never imagine. Rollo May once described compassion as being in a music shop, and plucking a single string of one violin. Then, the same string on all the other violins in the shop begins to resonate.

It is the willingness to receive and *be* received that is the most fulfilling and enduring of our shared moments. Through our willingness to participate in and to witness each other's growth, we become guardians of each other's souls, guides for each other's journeys. Then we can lead

each other into the light as well as into the dark places—
the abyss of old hurts, childhood wounds, and long-held
fears, which must be illuminated and understood if we are
to grow.

The poet Rainer Maria Rilke wrote: "For one human
being to love another; that is perhaps the most difficult of
all our tasks, the ultimate, the last test and proof, the work
for which all other work is but preparation." I often find
that the degree to which I am able to accomplish this labor
of love is proportional to the degree of importance that I
give to it; that the expression of love is the highest priority
and good that we can accomplish while we are here on
earth.

Love is there—always. It lives as we live. This is the
essence that gives breath to our bodies and to our souls.
This is the breath of God. It infuses each of us with life
and purpose. It endows us with the grace to give and receive the way our bodies breathe out and breathe in. In the
end, the measure of our lives will be the sum total of the
love that we have shared; of those selfless, loving moments that coalesce to define a life whose marrow and being is the expression of our birthright.

The Smoke Around the Heart

by *Joan Borysenko, Ph.D.*

"People want to be of service but worry about being selfish. Yet if you're not of service to yourself, you are being selfish, because you'll never be able in a loving way to connect with a larger network, let alone with one other person."

IT'S AN INVIOLABLE LAW. And that's the nicest part about it: What you give, you also receive.

I recently attended the wedding shower of a friend. In her midforties, she was marrying for the first time. In the perennial optimism of marriage, it was hoped to be the only time. There were about a dozen women there, and in what I thought was a sweet as well as useful idea, we were all asked to comment on what the most critical aspect of a loving relationship is.

It was as fascinating to hear what others said — each in her turn serious, funny, or outright ribald — as it was to wonder what would come to me when my turn came.

What I tried to say is this: *One of the most important aspects of a loving relationship is gratitude to the other for the gifts he or she bestows.* And this is a gratitude that must be acknowledged and must be spoken. It's vitally important to be constantly thanking other people for the loving things they do.

This act falls under the general category of what I call Not Taking Anything for Granted: not taking life for granted, not taking other people for granted, but recognizing that every time someone presents you with an act of kindness, he or she has given you a gift. It's a simple process of acknowledgment: Ah, this is a gift; it didn't have to be. And then thanking the person for it.

You need to stay alert to the fact that love itself is a gift. To receive it, you have to do something, like say, "Thanks." It's such a simple thing, like the old Shaker song, "Simple Gifts." Just because they're simple doesn't mean they're not valuable.

Another part of the giving and receiving of love is the importance of honesty and communication. Because often what passes for love is not love at all. An analogy is that what often passes for patience is not really patience at all but impatience, strained to its absolute limit. Frequently, what is considered loving is accepting from another things that are less than what you would wish them to be, yet not saying anything about it. Then you store up these moments, resentments build, and eventually stacks blow. This unspoken debris blocks the paths for both giving and receiving.

To keep the channels open and clear requires a willingness to talk about the things that are difficult. And that is hard for many people. It's hard to say something when you think someone else is not going to like hearing it. How could that be thought of as loving? But it is loving. And the more you can whittle down the time between the realization that something needs to be said and actually saying it, the better off you are. Honest communication is a skill, and it correlates with your ability to be able to truly give and receive love.

This notion is sometimes obscured in spirituality. When people think of spirituality, love, the sense of interconnectedness and loving-kindness, the ability to give and receive love, it gets a little fuzzy and sounds so wonderful. "I love you and you love me and, gee, isn't it all great?"

There are wonderful spiritual principles at work in this world, but it's too easy to forget the very basic psychological processes that are also a vital part of it. God, remember, lives in the details.

The details for everyone — but in some ways, I believe, particularly for women — are to learn to be self-aware, honest, and able to handle their emotional lives in a way that's going to be best for them. Then it will also work for others. Women tend to be very nurturing, very compassionate, very good at giving love. They are a little bit less good at receiving it in return. If they bury their own needs, they don't receive what they need and eventually start to build resentment about giving to others. Then they're in the bind that has many names, one of them being codependency.

The net result: They've given away themselves, and now there's nothing left. In their compassion and desire to help everybody, they lose themselves or fall into a rut of manipulation. But in the end, they find there's nothing left to give, no peace of mind, and all this goodwill has become pitched into a well of anger.

I'm often asked in workshops, "How is it that I can aim

for living a life of compassion and forgiveness, but wind up bitter, burned out, and codependent?"

Often we teach a kind of meditation in workshops that the Tibetan Buddhist tradition calls *Tonglen,* meaning the meditation of giving and receiving. It's a very graphic visualization exercise. You do it first for yourself, because Buddhists understand that unless you give something to yourself first, you won't have anything to give anybody else anyway. You have to take care of yourself first.

Then you do it for loved ones. Then you do it for people you might be in conflict with. And, gradually, you do it further and further out. If you were practicing the true Tibetan Buddhist method, you would do it for all the beings on all seven levels of creation.

First you visualize your own pain as smoke around your heart. You inhale that smoke into the light within your own heart and then when that smoke dissipates, you exhale your heart-light back to yourself. And you do that for others — breathing in their pain and breathing back your happiness, the wholeness of your own true nature. What tends to happen when people do this is, first, relief—because people inherently know that if they don't take care of themselves, there is no way to take care of anybody else.

But what's so wonderful about the Tibetan image is that when you compassionately take on the pain of someone else, you don't store it. It burns up, dissipates in your own heart, and leaves you with extra energy in the form of light; it illuminates you, even as you breathe it back at them.

The meditation exercise points up this basic psychological principle — that you need to make sure that you take care of yourself first. When you don't, the bind you get into is taking on others' pain and problems and then looking for your payback. So you walk around like an emotional beggar with your heart hanging out. And the recipients of your beneficence are disempowered and probably resentful.

Untangling this process is a serious problem, discovering the difference between truly giving and receiving love, and storing others' psychic pain or trying to fix their life. You can disempower them and injure yourself, because you've given without leaving enough for yourself.

There's a wonderful poem by Mary Oliver, "The Journey," which ends with the line that the only person you can save is yourself. Nothing could be truer. People want to be of service but worry about being selfish. Yet if you're not of service to yourself, you are being selfish, because you'll never be able in a loving way to connect with a larger network, let alone with one other person.

I wish there were a term other than *codependency*, because people tend to associate that word only with addiction. I think that codependency involves a much larger principle. You can tell that there's something wrong with the personal equation in a relationship if you don't feel enough love coming back to you. Again, it's a very simple thing, a "what's wrong with this picture?" scenario. But you need to look at the picture in two ways — directly at yourself and also at the situation.

It's like the notion of surrender in the Serenity Prayer, in which you ask for the serenity to accept the things you cannot change, the courage to change the things you can, and the wisdom to know the difference. If you look at your life and say, "Something's wrong; I'm pissed off all the time, and I'm not getting the love that I need," it would be ridiculous to add, "Well, gee, if everything was spiritually right, I could just surrender to this situation and keep loving everybody and feel fine."

It may be exactly the wrong tack to surrender to the situation. You may need to tell your friend to find somebody else to hang out with, you may need to get out of your marriage, or you may need to use tough love with your children. You can't tiptoe past the basic feedback of the psychological world in which we live, hoping to ascend to the larger, richer spiritual realm. Saying "If I just gave and received love properly, everything would fall into line" is a little too easy, I'm afraid. It's the old spiritual bypass routine.

It's not easy to learn to ask for what you need. It's not easy to ask a child, a friend, or a spouse for what you need. Nor is it easy for people to ask the Great Spirit, to ask the great mystery, for what they need, either. But it must be learned. I don't know an easy way of learning to do it, but we learn by doing. Just ask. The Great Spirit isn't a mind reader, and neither is your spouse.

I've always been in favor of recognizing the need for mucking around in the mines—learning the basic principles we need to deal with. Even the dark side has its lessons. Anger is a great teacher in learning to give and receive love, because it's pure feedback. It's a clanging gong that announces, "Something is radically wrong." The message may be painful, but it's also simple and clear.

The joyous message is also simple and clear. Being grateful, encouraging other people, saying "What you did made my life better" encourages others to do more of that, to be more loving—until, we hope, you're surrounded by encouraging people, who make you feel good simply being in their presence.

It's an inviolable law. And that's the nicest part about it: What you give, you also receive. The expression of gratitude is itself a simple gift. But the effect is huge: it creates more love in the world.

GOD IS LOVE

BY *Hugh and Gayle Prather*

"Indeed love heals, but being loved does not. Being loved merely holds the door open for healing, for happiness, for fulfillment, for 'getting our needs met.' But to walk through that door, we must love."

OURS IS THE first generation to blame our parents. Now we lead the way again in becoming the first generation to blame our children. To sum it all up, one final self-help book must be written: *I'm a Victim — You're Not.*

So when our attention turns to love, we quite consistently believe that the only love worth having is love that is directed at us. In all our relationships — social, romantic, political, parental — we are interested in only those who can commit to *us*, amuse *us*, meet *our* needs. We have turned the prayer of Saint Francis on its head. The doctrine of our times now reads "May I not so much seek to console, as to be consoled. To understand, as to be understood. To love, as to be loved. For it is in getting that I receive."

Even a casual look around at the devastated families, abandoned children, and betrayed friendships should make it plain that this approach does not work. How much more evidence do we need that some truths never change? Perhaps in the realm of the eternal, giving and receiving are simultaneous. But in the temporal world, giving comes first. This basic truth is at the heart of every major religion and mystical teaching that has come to earth over the last several thousand years. You experience love by loving. It is that simple.

It would be impossible for the two of us to talk about love in anything other than devotional terms. Trying to do otherwise would force us to leave out most of what we have learned in the past eighteen years of counseling families and especially what we have learned in the thirty-one years of our marriage, the most important lesson being the extraordinary potential of love to transform those who exercise it.

Let us give an example. After almost fifteen years of a marriage in which Gayle committed to Hugh, but Hugh played out his family's old pattern of disloyalty, Hugh finally started coming to his senses. He realized that he had in Gayle someone who truly loved him. In fact, Gayle was perhaps the only person in Hugh's life who had ever loved him unconditionally. And yet, despite having had someone stand by him for fifteen years, someone who saw the goodness in him more clearly than he saw it in himself, Hugh had remained basically untouched by this love.

How could that be? Doesn't love heal?

Indeed love heals, but being loved does not. Being loved merely holds the door open for healing, for happiness, for fulfillment, for "getting our needs met." But to walk through that door, we must love. If being loved healed, all creatures great and small would now be perfect, for God has loved them all and always will.

During the many years that Gayle was committed to Hugh, she grew spiritually, she was basically happy, and most of the damage she still carried from childhood was released. Hugh, who did little more during this time than devote himself to his own pleasure, did not grow spiritually, was not freed from the effects of his childhood, and was not only unhappy but was periodically suicidal. It was not until Hugh committed to Gayle and, yes — as codependent as it sounds — put Gayle's happiness first that Hugh was finally healed of his destructive pattern.

Please remember that this occurred many years after the honeymoon period. Gayle no longer had youth. She never had money. She was merely a person. But a funny thing happens when we love a person — any person. We are acting a little like God. And when we act a little like God, we feel a little like God.

At that fifteen-year juncture in our marriage, we made a joint decision never to leave each other, never even to threaten to leave — no matter how angry we became. And we set aside time each day to work on various aspects of our relationship. We made these work sessions sacred and tried never to skip or interrupt one. We don't think it's a coincidence that within weeks of making this commitment, we both began to feel God's presence and that a few months later our first child was born.

Everyone is well acquainted with the fear of "loving too much." For example, people fear that having a life partner demands endless sacrifice: no more free evenings and weekends. No more leaving and returning as they wish.

No more spending money on themselves alone. No more time to pursue their long-term goals. In short, no more *them*. Yet once they have abandoned their dreams and succumbed to having a permanent partner, they discover that their fears are just beginning. For now comes parenthood. A mistake in their child's nutrition could lead to a fatal illness. A mistake in discipline could create a sociopath. A mistake in education could wipe out entire career opportunities. As their children mature, people worry that if they don't push them out of the nest quickly enough, sons will be emasculated and daughters will become "caregivers."

Most little children not only love their parents but know with all their being that their parents love them. In working with families in which there is abuse, time and again we have been awed by how powerful is children's perception of the spiritual bond between themselves and their parents. Even when they are being horrendously mistreated, these little ones refuse to believe that their parents do not love them. We have observed that the amount and duration of abuse necessary to convince these kids otherwise amazes and inspires us all over again.

Judging by how many adults seek to go back and reconnect with parents who abandoned them, searching sometimes for years to locate them, we suspect that the spiritual knowledge of the connection between two people is never completely lost to anyone. It's interesting how often the adults who undertake this search are happy with how their adopted or foster parents have treated them. Being raised lovingly appears to make people *more* likely to seek out other love connections. These adult children often do not have even childhood memories of the lost parent, but they will say, as one man was recently quoted in our local paper,

"I will always think of my adoptive mother who raised me as my real mom, but I still want to find my natural mother." The untouchable connection between spirit and spirit, between soul and soul, between God and the children of God, is a gentle memory that lies quietly in every heart. When we choose to do so, we can awaken it and know love.

Although the following attitude is no longer prevalent in most hospitals, in the 1970s when we started our support group for parents who were grieving the loss of a child, hospital personnel often discouraged parents from "getting too attached" to a baby who was dying, explaining that there was really nothing that could be done for their baby and that if they allowed themselves to become deeply bonded to the child, the loss when the child died would only be that much more painful.

However, some parents chose not to take this advice, instead devoting themselves in every possible way to loving their infant daughter or son. They would touch them, feed them if allowed to, pray for them, or just stay in the hospital and watch over them. In our grief-support group we noticed a marked difference between those parents who had held back on their love and those who hadn't. Contrary to what was predicted, the feeling of loss was much greater for the moms or dads who had distanced themselves, and their grief was particularly resistant to healing. But the parents who had loved without caution healed quickly and usually turned immediately to helping other parents. They were also much more likely to feel the comforting presence of their child in their daily life. They either knew or came to know that it was something much more than the child's body that they loved.

Does any of this mean that because we love someone,

we now must give up all the things we like to do? Does it mean we must let our spouse, our child, our parent, or our boss become a tyrant, the cruel princess or prince of our kingdom? Does it mean that every whim and proclivity of our partner or our kids somehow carries more wisdom or spiritual correctness than our own thoughts and desires? Obviously not. But it does mean that there will be many times when it will *appear* that we must sacrifice our plans for the welfare of someone else.

The mistake we are now making is in thinking we know what love *looks* like. Love isn't getting on our hands and knees, wiping up the footprints of a saint. It isn't necessarily more loving to say yes than to say no, to be submissive than to be firm, to disregard our own needs than to meet them. In fact, loving is not a behavior at all; it is a quality of the heart and mind. But the fear we now have about that quality is crippling our chances for personal happiness and growth. It is, in fact, keeping us from experiencing God.

Eventually, we see that where we expected sacrifice, our love laid a gift; where we expected boredom, our love laid a new interest; where we expected a dead-end day, our love transformed it into fulfillment. In making these seemingly endless sacrifices, we received a reality far more lasting than had we gone about our usual loveless life in our usual loveless way.

God is the river of light in which we all bathe. This brilliance flows through the core of every living thing. Nothing within the warring, separated images of the world reflects the unity of God, and yet the unseen waters of love surround us in all circumstances — no matter how petty or shameful or tragic they may be.

The uncomplicated reason that the experience of God must follow our decision to make another person's happiness as important as our own is that God *is* oneness. God is what creates and sustains and joins the spirit. God is our shared heart and mind. Although within the world God goes unrecognized, those who see their oneness with just one other living thing cannot fail to see God.

Loving Inside Out

by *Patricia Love, Ed.D.*

"I believe that we invite people into our lives, especially our partners, to be our teachers. The irony of this is that, having invited them to be our teachers, we then go kicking and screaming into the classroom!"

FILLING MY LIFE with love starts with controlling my mind. Over the years, I have learned that I possess not only an active mind but a slippery one. If I'm not attentive, my mind can drift to wherever there is energy, sometimes toward the negative areas. For years I drove myself with negative energy, constantly criticizing myself for what I was doing wrong. It has been a continual process of discovering that I have a choice about how I see myself and my life, how I feel about things. The more positive choices I make, the more love flows freely into my life.

Now I understand that self-love is about honoring ourselves, literally actualizing the love in our life in ways that are unique and real to us. I have learned that I must love myself first. This has become a conscious task and, at times, a very difficult one. One day at a time, I still have to focus my deliberate intention to offset my history, to remind myself that I am lovable and loved.

The outcome of nurturing this internal fullness is love; I get full, then the people who are close to me get full. I am present for them, raw and fresh. Living this way has freed me to be a conduit, a channel for love to flow through to others and then back to me. Anyone can do this with her or his life. Just trust the process, stay with it, and understand that it doesn't always work in an orderly fashion.

I believe that we invite people into our lives, especially our partners, to be our teachers. The irony of this is that, having invited them to be our teachers, we then go kicking and screaming into the classroom! But if we can trust our choice, and trust the progress of our education, we can learn much as we follow the path that our partners lay out for us. Our partners are in a unique position to give us an invitation into ourselves, lead us into our blind spots.

One way that our partners offer us teachings is through sexual intimacy. This is a unique contribution our partners make and can continue to make through all our years together. Yet sometimes we forget that after the initial physical passion fades, there is something deeper to create, to allow to unfold. So often we lose out on this wonderful teaching place of trust and love and mutually discovered wisdom because we get lost in how to communicate our needs and desires. Without a way to understand each other, we get bogged down in lost expectations and misunderstandings. We need to listen to our partners, truly listen, to allow the intimacy to grow. If we can find a way to do this, we will know a deep peacefulness that comes from the growth of love and trust and shared history. The commitment, the loyalty, the love we share can create a unique well of love to draw upon for all the areas of life.

The lessons our partners teach also come from areas of apparent conflict. One of the things I find in my own practice is that the partners often have their own answers, for the relationship, for themselves, and for each other. They just need a midwife to birth the solutions, a safe environment in which to listen for the lessons. Ironically, if we can let ourselves listen, truly listen to what our mates are telling us, move beyond the style or the tone or the particular words, we may hear that they are speaking some piece of our own truth. Listening for this message is a difficult, humbling task, but if we can let down our walls enough to let it happen, we achieve new and ever-deepening intimacy.

Communication is essential in creating intimacy. We need to open ourselves to the real messages our partners are sending us, not only about ourselves but about the partners' own needs and desires. When we can receive the true messages and respond unselfishly sometimes, focusing on our mates' needs, we find deep and lasting partner-love. When this happens around sexual needs and practices, greater fulfillment results. But it needs to happen outside the bedroom as well. The partners need to connect regularly throughout each day, freely and fully sharing thoughts, feelings, dreams, and desires. We may still need to discuss who should pay what bill when, but we shouldn't forget to give a little hug and little kiss as we're passing by! In the same way that we listen more freely, less critically, we need to speak more carefully, choose our words more wisely. So often I have seen how couples get caught up in the feeling of the moment, forgetting to measure their words. The sparks fly, and the message gets lost. Learning to communicate carefully is work — hard work. It may be the hardest work we ever do. But all relationships involve work. There are no perfect partners, no perfect relationships. There are relationships, though, in which the partners' needs are met, in which the bond is nourished and therefore endures and provides the teaching that keeps us ever-growing.

Another feature of a deep and meaningful relationship is a willingness of the partners to let the other take center stage sometimes. To be mindful not only of our own needs but of our partners', to be willing to put the other first sometimes, is an essential part of creating a loving, enduring bond. Sincere and loving sacrifice is a beautiful, necessary gift: we may, for example, decide to make love even when we don't feel like it, just because our partners need us. By the same token, our mates may sometimes decide to respect our requirement for solitude, even when they want closeness just then.

Of course, even though we admit our partners into our lives as teachers, we don't follow blindly. Doing so would be as destructive as ignoring their role in our own development as people. We must learn to trust our own inner wisdom. For years I denied my intuition, my gut feelings, and my mental acuity. It was a terrible, painful deprivation that I've worked to overcome. We all need to trust our own minds, our own feelings, our own emotions, our senses, and our bodies. When we do so, there is a wonderful blending of the inner and the outer. We can become receptive to our partners, and the lessons they have for us.

Some people find themselves continually rejecting the lessons their partners and the people close to them offer. They feel that others are letting them down. Sometimes our loved ones do fail us, but just as often the gap may actually be caused by our own lack of self-trust. If we keep saying, "I trust these people and they keep disappointing me," then it may be that we are actually disappointing ourselves. If we are out of harmony with ourselves, not listening to our own inner whisperings about what is safe and true, the proper messages can't get through. And we feel let down.

When we deny ourselves the benefits of our own inner wisdom, we deny ourselves self-love and self-care, and we're less effective and fulfilled in our own lives — for what we are blind to in ourselves, we are blind to in others. But when we tune in to our own deepest messages, we can create a space of love around us and can live in a context of love that nurtures not only ourselves but the world.

THE MIRROR OF LOVE

BY *Harville Hendrix, Ph.D.*

*"One of my favorite sayings is that love does not cre-
ate marriage — intentional, conscious marriage creates
love. The same is true in all relationships. Love is born
in the midst of conflict. And this is how we have been
able to keep the dream of love and romance alive."*

MY WIFE, HELEN, and I have known each
other for eighteen years and have been married for thirteen. Recently, we were asked to
present a keynote address on the subject of "keeping the
dream alive." We were asked to talk about our relationship and the techniques we have devised to keep our love
growing and thriving. At first, Helen and I were intimi-
dated — we certainly didn't want to present ourselves as
models, but we also didn't want to present ourselves as too
flawed. Finally, we decided we'd just tell the truth — that
our current relationship is the result of thirteen years of
struggle, years that have been every bit as challenging for
us as for anybody else.

One of the major difficulties that we encountered over the years was an inability to make romantic moments last. It seemed that every time we created a romantic moment, whether it was reading poetry to each other, going to a movie, or having dinner at a fine restaurant, we just couldn't seem to hold it. It would last for that evening, maybe — but we would definitely blow it within a few days, if not that very night. Then we'd be back into tension with each other. So, at a certain point, we both just stopped trying to be romantic. Why work at what wasn't working?

Once we realized what was happening, we began to look at our relationship with a critical eye. We found that our romantic moments were sabotaged when we became analytical of a trait or behavior in the other person. For instance, we would have different points of view about a movie and we'd show little appreciation for the other's ideas. We would criticize each other. And then we made an interesting discovery: we each possessed the very same traits that we criticized in the other. And not wanting to accept a particular disliked trait in ourselves, we would assign it to the other. We came to understand that rejection of a trait or behavior in the other was actually a form of self-rejection. We concluded that unconscious self-hatred was the source of our conflict and probably fueled the power struggles of many (if not all) couples.

Not only does this unconscious self-hatred get in the way of expressing love, it also interferes with receiving love. You cannot feel worthy of accepting love if you unconsciously hate yourself or even hate some parts of yourself. We finally realized that in order to increase our self-love, we had to learn to love in the other person the trait we most disliked in ourselves. And we had to stop criticizing each other, because the more we criticized a disliked trait in the other, the more we increased our unconscious self-hatred. We theorized that the deeper recesses of the brain aren't able to distinguish between the inside and the outside, and so they receive the acceptance and love that we give to each other as if it were self-love. It also translates our criticisms of each other into self-rejection. Putting it all together, we came to the conclusion that self-love is the paradoxical achievement of loving another, *especially* that part of the other which we reject in ourselves.

To this end, we created a system for developing what we call a conscious marriage. In such a relationship, conflict that usually tears apart couples is reframed as an unconscious attempt to resolve issues and connect at a deeper level. Criticism, the coercive language of conflict, creates defense and distance rather than contact. What people need to do as couples is to cooperate with their unconscious, which is trying to maintain the couple's essential connection and restore their original wholeness. To do so, we developed a special form of communication that we believe is essential to any relationship, especially a loving one. This process is called intentional dialogue and was inspired by the Jewish philosopher and theologian Martin Buber.

The process includes three steps. The first step involves what we call direct mirroring. It is designed to help the listener hear the other person without any interpretation or emotional reaction: the listener merely reflects back the speaker's words. All emotional interpretations of what the words mean are dropped. The listener merely paraphrases back to the speaker what the speaker just said, *without judgment.*

Step two is what I call validation. Once the listener has heard the other person without adding any interpretation, he or she then must try to see the issue from the other's point of view. An example could sound something like, "What you are saying to me makes sense, *because* . . ." Then the listener completes the sentence, filling in the blanks after *because*. Another example: "Given the fact that I was late, it makes sense to me that you would think I didn't care or that I didn't take my obligation seriously." This statement forces the listener to see that the logic in the other person's mind is equal in value and truth to the logic and truth in his or her own mind. It's a very self-transcendent act and a great equalizer!

The third part of the dialogue process is empathic relating, or truly understanding the partner's feelings. When you are able to mirror the feelings of the other person, validate the other, and see through his or her eyes, then you have become empathic. An instance of empathic relating: "Given the sense of what you are experiencing, I can imagine that you must feel hurt or excited or angry." Amazingly, if you keep practicing empathic behavior, you find that you eventually begin to experience the actual feelings and inner world of the other person. Through empathy, you share the center and experience of your essential connectedness while retaining your unique individuality. We call it freeing the partner from the prison of our conceptions.

Helen and I, with the help of Buber, see this process as discovering the "thou-ness" of the other person without surrendering the "I-ness" of yourself. I am not really capable of loving you until I surrender my position that my way is the right way, until I can see the logic of the way your mind works, and until I can experience your feelings as yours, separate from mine. It's when I can truly see and experience your "thou-ness" that I can begin to love. Up to that point, what I may profess to love is actually what I imagine you to be. I am only really loving my own representation and therefore am really only loving myself. True love is when I can experience and honor your otherness, apart from my needs and expectations. And I can maintain that love, even though my experience of you may not always be either satisfying to me or a way to serve my needs.

We have also been able to use this process when dealing with our children. Just recently, I was frustrated with Hunter, who is ten, and began to express my feelings in a strong way. Instead of reacting by defending himself, he began to mirror my thoughts and feelings, which rapidly brought the tension to an end. Another time, during a car trip, I was expressing some anger to my wife about something she had done. My daughter Leah then leaned over the front seat and whispered into Helen's ear, "Mirror him, Mom." That effectively ended the scene! But the best part of all this is that the level of emotional connection between Helen and me is now being experienced by our children.

Helen and I also use intentional dialogue with our adult children. Whenever they are upset with us, we invite them into dialogue. The conversation sometimes is very long, but it always ends with connection rather than conflict, distance, and alienation. The dialogue process creates such a level of connectedness that the energy just flows.

You can also use this process for responding to positive experiences, not just conflictual ones, and it enhances the communication and deepens the connection between you and the other person. Mirroring the positive reinforces the experience — in turn reinforcing the behavior that brought about the good experience in the first place.

In my work and in my life I have seen how feelings of being unloved have more to do with a person's own unconscious self-hatred and self-rejection than with a true absence of love. These unconscious feelings can make it impossible for someone to take in any information that counters them — namely, that the person is loved. So the question is, How can you get in touch with your unconscious self-hatred and begin to modulate it?

You can do this by becoming aware of what you really don't like in your partner or your children or in humankind in general. What is it that really bugs you? I find that I get annoyed when my wife, Helen, overindulges in sweets or spends what I think is too much time on the telephone. But then I also sometimes overindulge or withdraw from people by spending too much time on the computer. Once you can truthfully figure out what bothers you in other people, you probably have accessed your own self-hatred, which has then been projected on someone else.

How do you transcend this projection? I have found that I can learn from looking at the function of a behavior in Helen's life (let's say, talking on the telephone) and seeing what it means for my life. Then I try to figure out if there's some part of my own behavior that is like hers (being on the computer too long). If I reframe Helen's behavior as functional for her, serving her in an important way, and value it — even support it and love it — I can then begin to experience what I call parallel self-love. While I am loving her, I am also loving myself. I have bypassed the unconscious self-hatred. Every time I look at another person without judgment but with understanding and empathy, I am doing the same thing for myself. The result is that I experience the love I give.

As we have increased our own self-love through loving each other, we have found that we don't need to set up romantic events and times to express our love. We have created a safe place and, as a result, feel romantic all the time. If we get too busy, then we can just go back to the intentional dialogue system and give ourselves some time to reconnect. And there doesn't have to be a conflict for us to communicate in this way. It is my belief that it's in the safe space of seeing the other as a "thou" that love is born and sustained. One of my favorite sayings is that love does not create marriage — intentional, conscious marriage creates love. The same is true in all relationships. Love is born in the midst of conflict. And this is how we have been able to keep the dream of love and romance alive.

4.

Love Is a Verb

"The love we give away is the only love we keep."

— ELBERT HUBBARD (1859 – 1915)

LISTENING

FOR LOVE

BY *James and Salle Merrill Redfield*

"When our intention is geared toward love, when we trust that the deeper, mystical part of us is always lying beneath these negative feelings waiting for a chance to surface, the letting go becomes easier. It's almost as though we're getting out of our own way so that we can come back to this mystical state of love, this most natural state of being."

BRINGING LOVE INTO your life is the way to lead the most fulfilling life. Love is the force, the energy that animates creativity and peace in each one of us. And on the collective level, when we center ourselves and bring love into our being, we engage in the historical process, in purposeful evolution.

History is all about trying to pull more and more love into the physical dimension. Throughout the whole story of human civilization, we see watershed moments in which more love, understanding, and connectedness — and, consequently, more peace—have been brought into our world. This happens as each person brings more and more love into his or her everyday consciousness, not just when he or she thinks about it or when someone brings up the subject, but as an ongoing state of being. As more people act lovingly, they bring even more love into the world. Loving, we believe, is the very purpose of human existence.

Our opportunities for healing the world have grown even greater. Technology has created a smaller world, a smaller community for humanity. We're all so much closer together than ever before. It's more difficult to deny the pain that exists elsewhere. The pain in the war-torn parts of the world is really our own pain, a pain that we all share. Our own individual actions are extremely important because we are all part of this larger matrix, a global web. Our own acts of love build energy that we can all draw upon. Even a little bit of love on our part can create an important foundation for future generations to build upon.

In our own personal lives, we bring in love in two ways: by actively seeking it and by clearing the way for it to come. This is an everyday process. When the two of us wake up in the morning we try to express how much love we are feeling. If we're slamming doors and "kicking the dog," it means there is some frustration and irritation in ourselves that needs to be cleared. At that point, when we're honest and address our feelings, it simply becomes a matter of "letting go," which clears the way and allows the love to return.

How do we "let go" and clear the way? By being completely honest, fully acknowledging our feelings, no matter what they are, no matter how nonloving they might be.

It is only when we are fully conscious of our feelings that we can process them and let them go. When we recognize negative feelings — instead of denying them — they can pass through us, thereby clearing the way for love to re-enter our lives. The two of us transcend our own negativity by making sure we're not identifying with it. We all have nonloving as well as loving feelings within us, but the nonloving part of ourselves is not the "true self." The true, or higher, part of the self is always seeking the state that mystics talk about, the state in which we are filled with a universal love and a peaceful euphoria.

The key to this state of mind lies in letting go and accepting whatever is happening in our lives at the moment. This acceptance doesn't mean we can't or shouldn't strive to be in a different place or to improve our life. Everyone's life is always flowing, and we all need to participate in the forward movement. But, at the same time, we need to accept whatever is in the moment.

Most of our frustration, anger, and nonlove in life is the result of wanting life to be different. We need to recognize and accept these feelings — and then let them go. (It's simple — but not easy!) If we identify with our negative, nonloving feelings, if we dwell on them and hold on to them, if we believe that they are all we have, it's extremely difficult to release them. But when our intention is geared toward love, when we trust that the deeper, mystical part of us is always lying beneath these negative feelings waiting for a chance to surface, the letting go becomes easier. It's almost as though we're getting out of our own way so that we can come back to this mystical state of love, this most natural state of being. Life is a continual process of first noticing and accepting what interferes with our loving feelings, then allowing the negative to leave so that the love can return. This is a day-to-day, moment-to-moment experience. As we trust in the process, we open ourselves to greater and greater amounts of love.

We can help others in this process, as they can help us, and so, actively bring love into our lives. Listening — really listening — is a critical part of filling our lives, and the world, with love. It's important to listen at a deep level to those around us and to enter into a dialogue with them, validating what they are saying. The more we listen in this fashion, the greater the love, respect, and compassion we feel for one another. Sometimes we are in such a hurry that we forget where the other person is coming from — are they hurt, confused, angry, or in need of love? Slowing down and listening lets us hear the truth in the moment. And it's the key to better understanding others and ourselves.

Try this powerful exercise: find someone whom you can really listen to, and who will listen to you, and ask him or her to simply sit quietly with you and repeat back what you say. This simple act of hearing your own words mirrored back, perhaps as much as anything else, allows you to feel truly heard and understood. (You will probably then want to let the other person have a turn, with you reflecting back his or her words.)

Developing listening skills is especially helpful in dealing with another person's anger. If we're angry at each other but take the time to slow down and really pay attention to what is happening within the person with whom we are in conflict, almost without exception we can say to ourselves, "I've felt that way, too." That realization enables us to bring forth our compassion and understanding in almost any situation. We can say to ourselves, "She's not a terrible, mean person, as it might seem on the surface, but rather a person in pain who needs love." Staying in this loving, listening frame of mind — and staying out of the negative — gives us the clarity to solve problems rather than latch onto them and make them worse. On a personal level, this type of listening keeps the two of us very bonded and connected. It's difficult at times, particularly if we're disagreeing, but that is when we need it most.

Similarly, an interaction may be driven by what is going on inside ourselves. We may see this in the rise of judgmental, nonloving thoughts. When we can let go of these negative thoughts and feelings, we can stop blaming the other person and re-ignite our own loving feelings that, in turn, allow us to truly love this person. Then we have the power to change the situation, because we have changed ourselves. If we wait for the other person to change first, we're missing the opportunity to grow and to expand our own love. (And we're setting ourselves up for disappointment! Each of us is on his or her own journey, responsible for his or her own course corrections; we can only change ourselves, not others.) Love, remember, comes from inside of us. It's not something we wait to get. The amount of love that we have inside ourselves defines the amount we can give to others. So, in a sense, the most important inner work is simply learning to love ourselves fully. This allows us to do our part in filling the world with love.

Even horrible situations can be seen as opportunities to learn more about our own nonloving ways. When we take a look at the hatred around the world, we can see that we all have prejudices, anger, and mistrust we need to let go. We can all make a difference on the global level by working on ourselves as individuals. The anger in ourselves can be replaced with love. As we awaken to ever-present love, we can begin to visualize this love expanding into other parts of the world.

A natural extension of filling our lives with love is not trying to control where life is going. And then, something synchronistic occurs — someone calls, we get an inspired idea to pursue that day, we cross paths with someone we haven't seen in years. Once we let go, our higher selves take over and life takes its own course. Days become more productive, creative, enjoyable, and filled with wonderful, mysterious events.

As the process continues, we get in touch with whatever our greatest contribution might be. This is different for everybody. Some of us might lead prayer vigils for the war-torn parts of the world. Others might raise our children, transform our given occupation, or simply smile at our customers. No one's contribution is more important than anyone else's. We're all simply doing what we're led to do by our higher selves. And we make our best contribution to the ongoing spiritual evolution of the world.

The love we all want is available. It starts within us, but it's everywhere else, too. "Seek and you will find." Don't be willing to accept an ordinary life and don't be willing to accept the models of our previous generations. We have the potential to transcend and break through previous forms of negativity by redefining reality and what we believe possible. If we look for love, we will surely find it. At first it can take some "faking it till you make it," meaning that filling our lives with love begins with the intention to do so as well as knowing that it is possible. And as we hold on to this vision, and work with it, the experiences we are looking for begin to enter our lives. Have patience, let go — and love will happen.

Love Wins

by *Samahria Lyte Kaufman*

"Living love passionately — and the key word is pas-sionately — creates joy all around us. The passion ig-nites the love into flames that are seen and felt by anyone with whom we're engaged."

W E LOVE ONLY to the extent that we ourselves are happy. Before we can truly love an-other, we have to learn to love and accept ourselves. For me this process was difficult, as I did not love myself at all.

I took the first step when I began to cease judging those negative characteristics I perceived in myself. I began to learn to accept who and how I was, without needing to change all these things. Once I accepted an aspect of my-self, then changing it was much easier. I realized I was at every moment doing the best I could.

I decided that the power for creating my own happi-ness — my own unhappiness as well — was in my hands and no one else's. This power was not dependent upon what others said or the situations that arose in my life. I was not a victim, but in fact a creator.

I made happiness and love my first priority — even before I got what I wanted in any given situation or knew whether life was going to work out the way I thought best. Like the carrot in front of the horse, I held this priority before my eyes, and this focus helped me change myself. With each change I made, I became happier; and the happier I became, the more loving I was.

An example of how powerful these changes can be involves the story of my son, Raun. At eighteen months old, Raun was diagnosed as autistic. The slide into autism took about six months, during which time he went from a child who looked at everyone, laughing and enjoying his interactions with people, to a child who was completely disconnected from people.

We sought out everybody we could to research what treatments were being done with autistic children. The main form of therapy back then was — and is still today — behavior modification. We saw that these children's behaviors were being judged as bad and inappropriate. We didn't feel that way about Raun. Our conclusion was that he was acting in this manner because he needed to; he must be taking care of himself in some way.

With that in mind, I began to work with him myself, twelve hours a day, seven days a week, for three and a half years. At that time he was diagnosed as autistic but also as having an I.Q. below 30, and he was totally mute and unresponsive. Just a few months ago, at age twenty-two, Raun graduated from Brown University with a degree in biomedical ethics.

Every time I think about this transformation, I realize it was a miracle made possible because of love. Had I not worked on my own heart so dramatically to learn how to be happy and love myself, I would not have been able to love and, most important, to accept him exactly as he was.

I have a daily practice that helps me create a more loving way of dealing with the world. When I begin to feel even the slightest bit uncomfortable or challenged, I do one of two things. I first question myself to determine what is happening and how I am feeling about it. Then I ask if there is anything that I think I'm going to get from this discomfort. This self-questioning helps me to uncover previously held beliefs that might be counterproductive or even hurtful to who I am now. Once I discover these beliefs that are causing the pain or unhappiness, I can choose to keep or discard them. If I discard these old beliefs, I find my life becomes much more effective. Second, I can realize that what I want is to feel good and loving at that moment — and this becomes my first priority. Then I make that realization into a decision to feel loving.

I feel that when we love in the fullest way possible, without worrying whether our love is reciprocated equally, we are immensely rewarded. Thus, the one who loves the most, wins. It serves me well, because then I don't feel sorry for myself if I love someone more than he or she loves me.

I try to assume the best about people, which doesn't mean being naive. It means knowing that each person has a reason for whatever he or she is doing. We can give other people the benefit of the doubt and stay open to listening and trying to understand them.

It's important to express and demonstrate love — not

only in words but in actions, giving what's important and meaningful to the other person. Often people don't make their love tangible; they don't do the things that matter to the other person, so the other person doesn't *perceive* that he or she is loved.

If someone does something we don't like, we can see it as an opportunity to grow stronger and more loving. When I am dealing with someone who is angry or attacking, rather than seeing myself as put down or hurt by that person, I just say to myself, "This is an incredible opportunity for me; this is happening right now to benefit me." I can ask myself, "What am I going to do with it?" I can get angry right back, I can feel hurt, I can feel diminished in some way, or I can love more and try to express what I think and feel from a perspective of personal strength and power. So we actually use occasions where others are unhappy with us to empower ourselves to feel stronger and more loving. This has been so enlivening for me.

Love is a decision that we can make anytime under any condition, but first we have to know that it is a decision. Everyone wants to love more and be loved more — everyone. Just remember that opening up our awareness, even in a situation that doesn't feel so loving, can soften everything.

Everything I do is based on creating a happy, loving attitude toward myself and others. This is my main aim and focus. When we make our attitude the most important thing, we can inspire others and show by example what it's like to bring forth and share an attitude of love. When people really experience that attitude from another person, they want it for themselves. Living love passionately — and the key word is *passionately* — creates joy all around us. The passion ignites the love into flames that are seen and felt by anyone with whom we're engaged.

When we are more loving, we are more likely to create miracles in our lives. Part of this process is learning to stay present within each moment. Living in the present is very freeing and brings me immediate comfort. Another important ingredient is gratitude. Being grateful is a powerful tool in feeling love toward everything or everyone in our lives. The energy of love we emanate changes everything around us for the better. Person by person, moment to moment, as we love, we change the world.

A LOVING

PRESCRIPTION

BY *Andrew Weil, M.D.*

*"I doubt that there is much I could do to promote a more
loving way of dealing with the world if I weren't connected to that same loving force in myself. Thus, as with
so many areas of my life, the work begins within."*

I LIVE IN AN especially magical and remote area of the
Tucson Valley, bordering a national park. It's a wild
and spectacular place of natural beauty. I garden on my
land and work to maintain it as a beautiful place around
me. This activity helps me stay centered. And this beautiful place is where I meet my patients. Patients come to my
home, and I see them in a room that I live in.

It's far from town, so the trip is difficult for some. Patients arrive with much anticipation and expectation. But I
don't really receive them as a doctor. I relate to my patients on a very personal level. I don't use any of the for-
malities that people usually associate with doctors.

Possibly I belabor the old "physician, heal thyself" line,
but I doubt that there is much I could do to promote a

more loving way of dealing with the world if I weren't connected to that same loving force in myself. Thus, as with so many areas of my life, the work begins within.

My mornings begin in meditation. It's something I do when I first arise, to help keep me centered for the day and able to deal with whatever comes along. It's not hard for me to remember the time before I used to meditate, a time when my moods were far more erratic than they are now.

Part of my meditation is the Buddhist heart meditation. The heart meditation is to imagine filling your heart with love, and then expanding that love out in ever-widening circles. First, open your heart to your immediate vicinity and to the people in your community. Then send love out to the state, to the country, and eventually to the entire world. It is a visual and mental meditation. When I do this practice, I go right through the evolutionary chain. First I cultivate plants and project a lot of love onto them. Then I relate to my pets. I feel great love for my dogs and parrot and send love to them. Next I relate to my children and stepchildren, and on it goes.

I know that my experience of the world is very much determined by my perceptions of it. My consciousness influences and also limits what I see. So by connecting to the source in myself that is loving, I am able to see the love around me. Then the resonance with others can begin.

I think that's what falling in love is all about — you're really projecting what you feel inside you onto another person or onto something out there. I think if people can recognize that this falling-in-love impulse comes from an inner source, then there's always a way of connecting with it — certainly not only in the romantic sense.

The true definition of healing is "to make whole." Too seldom are physicians trained to realize that the remedy can come not necessarily in the form of a pill but in an intangible ingredient we can only wish could be encapsulated.

Love is the one source of sustaining comfort in life, and it is of such force that it has miraculous powers of healing in the physical, mental, and spiritual realms. We must try to cultivate that force and to experience it as habitually as possible.

There's no doubt in my mind of the relationship between mental and emotional states and the state of our health and resistance to disease. I've seen it. A number of my patients have experienced the complete disappearance of chronic symptoms — including severe back pain and auto-immune diseases like lupus — through fortuitously falling in love. Being in a state of love releases such positive energies to flow freely around the body, it can cure any number of ailments.

Do I prescribe falling in love? In a way, I do — though obviously I can't send my patients to the pharmacy for this particular elixir. I often don't even talk directly to patients about love and loving. Yet it is always behind my ideas and my questions to them.

All physicians want to do well for their patients. Yet there is so little being taught to medical doctors today about emotional states and their influences on health. There's nothing about spiritual experiences and their influences on health. There's little about the art of medicine — including the art of listening, communication, and suggestion in the service of healing. I think doctors are relatively untrained in such areas, and I believe it would be healthier for everyone if this were changed.

I look at my patients not just as physical bodies but as mental and emotional beings as well. I am always thinking of suggestions to give them that might enable them to be in healthier mental states. These might be very specific, simple, sensible ideas, such as recommending that patients spend more time in nature, that they buy flowers and keep them in their environment, that they seek out the company of friends who make them feel good. I might recommend to some that they meditate. My suggestions are very individualized, depending on my sense of each patient, what they're open to, and what they're ready for.

Relationships are the greatest challenge that we face as human beings. If living one's own life is difficult, living with another person is incredibly difficult. Yet this is the way in which we really refine our personalities. We are thrown headfirst into all the areas of our deficiencies, forced to confront the many issues that we still need to learn. Yet it is because of this challenge that relationships become a part of our spiritual work.

Just as love flows from within and expands into widening circles, so relationships move in cyclical forms. There is something cyclical about the nature of love between people that allows people to fall away from love and then return to it. We keep recreating it. My wife and I experience this process when I find myself frequently on the road. During the separations, the homecomings tend to get better. I think this is part of the nature of a loving relationship. A relationship is constantly changing. And particularly over time, an underlying theme emerges: coming back together again and reexperiencing the other person in a way that is ever more loving throughout the years.

Eventually couples become families, and the challenge is sparked again. When we constantly live around people, and cycle in and out of other people's behavior (some of which can be very annoying at times), sometimes we have to withdraw from family interactions and get ourselves centered again before reentering the fray. For example, my breathing exercises are a useful emergency measure to help center myself. In our home we do some simple ceremonial rituals, and we're fairly physical—we hug a lot. All these family traditions and ceremonies serve to help us grow together.

And so does time alone, which is important and begins this cycle again. It is absolutely essential to carve out time for oneself. Otherwise, the swirling demands of daily life may obscure the crucial lesson: that all these inner reserves of love are easily accessible.

At any given moment, everything we need is there. All the lessons are there. All the love we need is there. We don't have to look outside ourselves; the source is within and always present, always there. If we can be open to that, and experience it, then we are fluent in the language of healing.

Drawing from the Well of Self-Love

BY *Louise L. Hay*

"No matter how much we give love, if we don't give it to ourselves, nobody can love us enough. If we are in relationships with people who don't have self-love, no matter how much we love them, it will never be enough because they are not giving it to themselves on the inside."

LOVE IS A natural thing; it is simply there, if we don't push it away. We are each born with love in us. Unfortunately, as we move through life, most of us accumulate blocks to loving. If we can just get the blocks out of the way, the love naturally fills our being.

If we don't fill our lives with love, we are miserable. Even though it is that simple, it still took me a long time to learn this. I used to be someone filled with resentment and self-pity, and I really didn't know what love was like. I thought it was something that I had to go out and find. It wasn't until I was able to let go of seeking love from the outside that I was able to understand what real love is.

I had to learn how to identify and push away my blocks to loving. Most of the blocks, I realized, had to do with my thinking. I am very aware that we can only think one thought at a time. So I refuse to think the negative thoughts that keep the love out. If I find those other thoughts creeping in, I just say to myself, "Louise, you don't have to think this way. You can think of something wonderful." Sometimes to break a flow of negative thoughts that is threatening, I repeat to myself simple words, such as *love, peace, joy, contentment,* and this act becomes enough to break my cycle of negative thinking. Then, automatically and unconsciously, the other loving thoughts come flowing in.

It's important for me to remember that I can choose to be happy. Most of all, I like to choose grateful thoughts because the more I am grateful for all the good things (I don't mean possessions but the joys of living), the more they come to me.

Many people contact me for help with health issues, even very serious ones. All I do is teach them to love themselves. They learn to look at what has gotten in the way of their love and health. Were they judging themselves as not being good enough? As they examine their beliefs in the light of reason, they often realize how silly those ideas are. I have people look into a mirror, just look into their own eyes, and say, "I love you." For most people, this is very difficult. So I immediately say, "Okay, what is wrong with you?" It always turns out to be some silly thing, like "My hips are too big" or "I am a bad person." "Okay," I ask, "why are you a bad person? What have you done?" Usually it is nothing, absolutely nothing.

So where do these thoughts come from? Mostly, it's old childhood voices that they carry with them. Many people are much better at giving love than at receiving love, because they don't feel worthy of receiving love. It comes down to the old "I am not good enough." That self-perception usually goes back either to some horrendous childhood incident or to just a relentless series of negative comments given to children over long periods of time. Society wants us to follow rules.

Society does not seek creativity; it demands conformity. In order to conform, people have to give up parts of themselves. Parents want little children to conform to their rules; then the children go to school and the school wants them to conform to its rules — and the individual becomes lost along the way. When we can adopt a sane viewpoint and really look at these things with a conscious mind, we find that there is really nothing in the way of love, and a huge weight drops off. I do believe that we have come to this planet to love ourselves in spite of whatever obstacles others or we ourselves have put in our paths.

Another way to bring more love into our lives is to be willing to forgive. That's a hard one. But lack of forgiveness locks up our hearts, keeps us in bitterness, holds us in resentment. It is a perfect breeding ground for self-pity. We can't love when we buy into all that. We have to look at all these negative thought patterns in the clear light, and learn to let them go.

When we let old thought patterns go, when we learn to forgive, we can love ourselves better. And when we love who we are, when we have self-worth and self-esteem, people will recognize that and treat us differently. Opening the channels to this universal energy brings good into our lives, and miracles literally happen. Good is out there, waiting to come into our lives, as long as we open ourselves to it. But if we close the doors with all the bitterness, the resentment, the anger, and the unforgiveness, our lives will be miserable and loveless.

We don't even need to go out and look for the good. We just have to release our own junk, the junk within us. When a person who eats lots of junk food decides to eat healthfully, over a period of time his or her health becomes stronger and stronger. That person hasn't really done anything, is not looking for help; he or she is simply taking care of his or her body. The junk goes out of the body and is eliminated. The same thing happens with our minds; as we eliminate the junk, the truth comes in.

One of the ways I actively bring love into my life is with my pet animals. I don't buy animals, I rescue them. All my animals have a history of abuse. But a year of love does wonders for all of them. What incredible changes are possible! I had one dog who was very difficult. Three times in the first three weeks she lived with me, I said, "I am going to take her back, I can't handle it." But a year later, this dog is my dream pet. People are no more complicated than animals. Get the fear out of the way, get the abuse out of the way, let people know they are loved and wanted and will be taken care of, and their true personalities come out.

However, there is one way in which people are different. For humans, self-love is the most important. No matter how much we give love, if we don't give it to ourselves, nobody can love us enough. If we are in relationships with people who don't have self-love, no matter how much we love them, it will never be enough because they are not giving it to themselves on the inside, and they will not trust ours. They can't let our love in because they haven't created a place to receive what we've offered, a place to receive love.

Once again, it's really as simple as loving ourselves. I am a very simple lady with very, very simple ideas about life. I always focus on looking for what stands in the way of the natural love flow and letting that obstacle go. Then we can start just to appreciate who we are and know that we are unique and special and wonderful and that there's nobody in the whole world like us, never has been and never will be.

Over the years I've developed my love rituals. I wake up in the morning with a little extra time to snuggle in bed. I say, "Oh, isn't this delicious and so comfortable and isn't it wonderful that I have this great bed to sleep in and the dogs that sleep with me!" Then I am practicing being grateful for the day. I always know that it is going to be a wonderful day and that there will be incredible experiences in it. Some of them I can expect, and some of them I cannot. I program my day with gratitude.

The last thing I do at night is also an expression of gratitude. Right before I go to sleep, I reaffirm what a wonderful day it had been. Sometimes the day would have included unpleasant experiences, but to me these are always about growth, so I am grateful for them as well.

Of course, everyone has crises. I have a little routine when a crisis occurs. As quickly as possible I say to myself, "All right now, out of this experience I know only good is coming. This is for my highest good, this is a wonderful experience, all is well, and I am safe." During a crisis I repeat this passage over and over, until my thoughts become clear. It's amazing: after practicing it a few times, the mind clears, and either a solution is found very quickly or something happens to allow the crisis to resolve itself.

Another thing I ask for every day is deeper understanding, so that I am able to see life's issues with more clarity. I think the people who create the most havoc in the world are people who once were abused as children and now have very little understanding of how life works. I am very aware that my thoughts and my words are creating my future. Knowing this, I carefully practice what I think, what I say, and what I do with other people. I know that what I give out will always come back to me. This doesn't mean that I never get angry. Everybody gets angry. But now my anger doesn't last the way it used to. Something that I used to stew about for three weeks now may take three minutes. And, consequently, I find that I have far fewer problems in my life.

I have also learned to give myself more love by working less. I used to work ten-hour days, seven days a week. I don't do that anymore. Mainly, I try my best to stay in my garden. I have a wonderful vegetable garden. I eat out of it as much as possible. I have fruit trees and lots of flowers and a pond with fish in it. I take care of it mostly by myself, because my gardening is my joy. I think I am just a farmer at heart.

Being overwhelmed by the details of our lives, by overwork, can squeeze the love out of our lives. I think it makes us terribly impatient. Recently I took two years off to restore my soul. I spent that time on my knees in my garden. I found I was giving so much to others that no matter how much I gave, it was never enough. I said, "Okay, I am going to decide how much I give." I suffered a lot of guilt. But I realized that I don't have to do it all; there are many wonderful teachers out there. As a teacher, I understand that my students must have many, many teachers, must study and learn from many people.

We each have to find our own way, balancing the details of our lives. But we all need love. My advice is to be loving and be very aware that everything we do and say and think is coming back to us. So if we love ourselves and love life and love everybody around us, we will find that our own lives will fill with an abundance of all that is good.

HEART TUGS

BY *Victoria Moran*

"You don't have to ponder the hows *and* whys *of what makes an act loving, or which situations contain the potential for love. When an opportunity to be loving presents itself, you know it. There is no doubt."*

I T IS CHALLENGING to talk about filling your life with love, for there is no single activity that can be called "showing love." It is easy, for example, to identify the activity of "washing dishes": that's the thing you do with dishes, soap, and water while standing at the kitchen sink. You're aware of what you are doing when you are washing dishes, and you are doing it deliberately.

Since there is no activity called "showing love," your love must be expressed in other ways, often through very mundane activities. You usually do not plan to be loving—you certainly don't make a notation in the daily schedule to be loving at 10:15. And often you're not aware of the fact that you are being loving.

If someone said, "Would you die for your child?" every parent would immediately reply, "Yes! Bring in the gurney, wheel me out of here." But suppose it's 8:00 at night, at the end of a long day. You're exhausted and your daughter asks, "Would you play chess with me?" When you drag your tired body and mind to the table for twenty minutes of chess, you are being loving.

Sometimes, many times, you do things that you really don't want to do at the moment, like playing with a child when you're tired and would prefer to just collapse into bed. You do these things because you are driven to do so by your love for the person, for humanity, for whatever touches your heart. And these acts of love, even if done reluctantly, help you to rise above your own problems and negativity.

I was given a tremendous lift by love some years ago when the woman who had helped to raise me was in the hospital, in a coma. One evening the doctor called and said, "I think we can save her with surgery. Can you come to the hospital now?"

I didn't want to go right then. You see, I had a history of food addiction. I had just begun recovery, and it was very important to me that I stuck to a regular eating schedule. I clung to those three meals a day because I didn't know what else to do. I thought they were my lifeline, but I was now being called on to be a lifeline for another human being. I even asked the doctor if I had to go to the hospital at that moment. He said, "Yes, come right now."

There was no question that I would go, but I worried about getting my next meal on schedule. After I had done what was required at the hospital and signed the papers, the doctor said, "It's going to be four or five hours. Why don't you go down to the cafeteria and get something to eat."

We went to the cafeteria, but it was closed; we had to eat dinner out of the vending machines. Here I was, just two months removed from binge eating, about to eat from the food addicts' slot machine! And yet, it was absolutely all right. I made the best choices possible from the ones available, and I got through that tense time without falling back into addiction. I was able to do so because my love for this woman, my acting out of that love, had lifted me above my own needs.

Just as the act of love can lift you above the problems of everyday life, actions can create love. One day, while waiting to get a massage, I saw two adorable little boys playing in the hallway. They had found a baby starling. The sensible approach would have been to mind my own business and keep my massage appointment, but I felt a tug in my heart. The bird needed care, so I said to the younger of the two boys, "Would you like me to take this bird to a bird doctor who can help it live?" The little five-year-old looked at me with his great big eyes and said, "I would really like that." Then he asked, "Will they bring it back?"

I replied, "We want this bird to be able to fly away and build a nest and have a family." That was harder for the little boy to accept, but he and his brother agreed, so I took the bird to a wildlife center, just across the state line in Kansas. The people there said, "Oh, this is a Missouri bird. We can't take a Missouri bird, that's against the law." They gave me the name of a wildlife center in Missouri to call, but it was after hours. Reluctantly, I took the bird home for the night.

The next morning I called the place in Missouri, but they said, "Starlings aren't protected in this state. If you bring it here, we'll have to euthanatize it." So I kept the young bird in my office at home, feeding it every two hours with soaked dry cat food and chopped blueberries. We have three cats and a bird dog, so we had to make my office into Fort Knox to keep them away from the little guy. We had to feed Chirpy as often as any baby. We couldn't go to the movies; we couldn't even be away from the house for more than two hours at a time. This responsibility was really a nuisance, but I became attached to the little bird. As much as I was thrilled to let Chirpy go and be a bird, I had fallen in love with him. Interacting with another being had created a great deal of love, even though the interaction was tedious and Chirpy had spent only eleven days in my world before being released to his own.

If someone were to ask me how to become a more loving person, I would simply tell him or her to follow the tugs that come from the heart. I think that everyone gets these gentle urges and should listen to them. Even if they sound absolutely insane, they may be worth going with. Recently my daughter and I were driving home from a health food store in a not very savory part of town. I make it a point to drive through any area of town that I jolly well feel like, because avoiding certain places is part of what makes them unsavory. Anyway, as we were approaching a stoplight, I saw a man dragging a woman down the street. At first, I thought that she was ill, that she was having some kind of seizure, and that he was helping her. But the looks on their faces, and the looks from the bystanders, gave a different impression.

I said, "Rachael, is that woman being attacked?" I was driving, so I couldn't quite see. Rachael craned her neck out the window, took a good look, and answered excitedly,

"Yes, yes, she's being attacked!" So I stopped at the red light, said, "Wait here," locked Rachael in the car, and went after the abused woman.

I have fairly extensive self-defense training. I know how to take care of myself if I have to, so I wasn't thinking over the situation. I was responding. I charged up to the man, who by that time had dragged the woman into a small office area. Everyone else was watching him, fearful, as I shouted at the top of my lungs, "Cut it out!"

Now, I'm a small person, in my midforties. I do not present an imposing physical threat. But the incongruity of the situation — this little person challenging a big guy — must have been powerful, because he just stood there, speechless. His mouth was moving, but nothing came out. I took a good look at the woman. Her face was red and swollen: she had obviously been punched. I continued, in a lower voice, "This woman looks as if she's in distress." He kept moving his mouth, but no words came out.

Then, to my surprise, the battered woman leaned over and kissed him on the cheek. This was evidently a he-beats-me-but-I-love-him-anyway situation. I had done my part, so I left. The rest was up to them.

As I returned to my car and drove away, I was filled with doubts. Did I want every thug in the city to have my license plate number? How could I have done this with my child in the car? But later, several people I respect told me that if they had been that woman, they would have wanted someone to step forward to help them.

The point of this story is not that I'm a hero or that I deserve a medal. Clearly, the battered woman didn't even want my help. The point is simply that you don't have to ponder the *hows* and *whys* of what makes an act loving, or which situations contain the potential for love. When an opportunity to be loving presents itself, you know it. There is no doubt. Whether it's returning a purse you find in the street, offering your seat to an elderly person on the bus, smiling at a clerk, or playing another game of chess with your child. Love is like a bell that's always ringing. All you have to do is listen. And the more you listen, the more you see opportunities to show love to others.

When I was at the lowest point of my life, I felt that I had only two things — and they weren't any publications or acclaim. One was taking care of Dede, the woman who had helped bring me up, during her difficult times. The other was the assistance that I had given to other people who suffered from food addictions. If I had died at that rock-bottom moment, I could have taken those two things with me to wherever it is that we go next. They were better than money or anything else. They were love.

Today, I would say that love is my religion. Love is the thing that I want permeating my life. Perhaps that is why Tibet is my favorite place to visit. The Tibetans have infused their everyday lives with spirituality and devotion. In Tibet you see people carrying out the ordinary business of life with their fingers on their prayer beads. They're praying along on their prayer beads as they barter in the marketplace, as they shop, as they carry their children on their backs. They walk while spinning prayer wheels, and their prayers go up to the heavens. Religion, spirituality, and everyday life are all entwined. For Tibetans, life, religion, and spirituality are all one thing, the same thing. Wouldn't it be nice to make life and love one and the same? To use everything as another opportunity to be loving?

It can be done. Life and love can be one. When you're loving people, you bring out the love within them. You may not see it every time, but the love you give gets passed along. It makes a chain that can transform the very nature of the world.

5.

A Gathering
of the Heart

*"There is no feeling in a human heart which
exists in that heart alone — which is not, in
some form or degree, in every heart."*

— GEORGE MACDONALD (1824–1905)

A Celebration

of Love

by *Leo Buscaglia, Ph.D.*

"In life and in love, there is only that moment, the now. The only reality we know is what we experience this very second. Reality is not what has passed or what has yet to come into being. Grabbing hold of this simple idea makes life magical because it brings love alive."

P
ERHAPS THE BEST WAY for us to fill our lives with love is to consider what love is all about. The act of loving is a continuing process of building upon the love that is already there — inside of us. Love is always present in all men and women. However, at every point in a person's life, love can be in a different stage of development. Love is always in the process of becoming.

Sometimes love may be difficult to recognize because it has a different manner of revealing itself to and through each person. To expect others to love in the same way you do at that moment is unrealistic and even foolish. Only you are you. Only you can respond to love, can give love, and can feel love as you do. The adventure lies in the discovery of love in yourself and in others. The excitement comes from understanding what love *is*, rather than what you insist it must be.

Cultures vary greatly in their attitudes toward displays of emotion. For example, when I visit my relatives in Italy, there is never any doubt about their love so sweetly and warmly expressed. I instantaneously feel their joy and excitement at my presence. I become caught up in their cries of happiness, their exclamations of love, the hugs, and the kisses. I am delighted with their emotional demonstrations, partially because I was raised with such noisy and physical outpourings of love. It's understandable, however, that this type of experience can be overwhelming or even frightening to those who are unaccustomed to such a showering of feeling.

Indeed, many people in our culture are extremely separated, especially physically, from others. In some parts of the world, both men and women kiss, embrace, walk hand in hand or arm in arm. In certain areas in the United States, however, this kind of behavior would be considered quite strange, if not illegal! I consider this attitude to be a shame, as touching can often be a form of communication far more powerful than mere speaking. To put your arm about another person, or on his or her shoulder, is a way of saying, "I feel with you," or "I care." Sadly, I have seen people crying while others can only look on in uneasy embarrassment. Someone may offer a handkerchief, but seldom an embrace. This does not mean that the uncomfortable onlookers are not loving people. They simply have limited means of expressing their love. The trick is to look past the cultural limitations to the true love that lies within and, most important, to encourage that love to bloom.

One of the more difficult concepts to grasp is that love lives in the present moment. Unfortunately, most of us are either stuck in yesterday or anxiously waiting for tomorrow. We have lost sight of the present moment.

Some look back fondly to "the good old days," trying to recreate past happiness and security. Others live strictly for tomorrow, spending their lives collecting achievements and external rewards in preparation for some grand tomorrow. We amass, or try to amass, great fortunes and store them away. We deny ourselves and our families daily to buy large insurance policies or other forms of future "security." Our lives are largely directed toward some nebulous future or perhaps even toward death itself. We are so concerned with tomorrow that we have lost sight of the purpose and potential joy of daily life and of loving today.

But we must remember that life is a process, not the goal. Life is all about striving to get there and enjoying the journey, not simply the arrival.

In life and in love, there is only that moment, the now. The only reality we know is what we experience this very second. Reality is not what has passed or what has yet to come into being. Grabbing hold of this simple idea makes life magical because it brings love alive. This understanding does not mean, however, that we should live for the moment. It does mean that we should strive to live *in* the moment, which is a very different thing.

Of course, the past has value and there are unknown treasures in the future. Only the moment, however, has true value, for it is here and can be lived fully. The rest is merely our imagination. Love knows this, for love does not look back. Instead, love experiences the past and takes the best from it. Nor does love look forward, for it realizes that tomorrow's dream remains awaiting and may never come. No, love is neither past nor present. Thankfully, love is now! And it is only in the *now* that love can be a reality. All else is but memory or hope.

There's an old Buddhist *koan* (a difficult question designed to force a student beyond logic toward illumination) that I shared in my book *LOVE*. This koan tells of a monk running from a hungry bear. He dashes to the edge of a cliff and stops, realizing that he must either jump or be eaten. He leaps off the cliff, but as he falls, he grabs hold of a small clump of wood jutting out from the face of the cliff. The poor monk looks down, only to see a starving tiger circling below, waiting for him to fall. Just at that moment, two hungry gophers on the side of the mountain begin to gnaw at the clump of wood from which he is suspended. The hungry bear is above, the starving tiger below, and the gophers are to his side. Looking beyond the gophers, he spies a wild strawberry bush and a giant, red, ripe, juicy berry within his reach, ready to be eaten. He plucks it, puts it in his mouth and eats it, exclaiming with delight, "How delicious!"

Such stories can teach us so much about where love resides — in the moment. Love revels in and grows in the moment. Love basks in the joy of the moment. As you immerse yourself in every moment, you discover more of what love wants to offer you. As a result, your life begins to fill with more love.

Adding love to life is always good. But as we fill our lives with love, we should consider the *type* of love we look to. The greatest love is what gives all, expecting nothing in return. Love is always willing, even delighted, to receive in return, but it never asks for anything — other than to be allowed to continue being. This is the purest love. It is also the most delightful love, for it can never be painful. You see, if nothing is expected in return, we can never be deceived or disappointed. Love can only be painful when it demands something in return.

The concept of pure love that gives without taking sounds simple, but its practice is not easy. Few of us are strong enough to give without expectations. But *real* love comes without strings attached. And it is only real love that is given without expectations.

If we love fully and deeply, then we have no choice but to believe, trust, accept, and hope that our love will be returned. But there are no guarantees. If we wait to love until certain of receiving equal love in return, we may wait forever. Indeed, if we love with any expectation whatsoever, we eventually are disappointed, for it's quite improbable that anyone is able to meet all of our needs, regardless of the strength of his or her love or devotion.

Buddhism teaches us that we move closer toward enlightenment when we cease desiring. Expecting something from others as our "right" is a prescription for unhappiness. Perhaps we can never totally surrender our wants, but the extent to which we can live without demands or expectations of others is the extent to which we are free from disillusionment and disappointment. Others give us only what they are able to, when they are able to, not necessarily what we desire them to give. When we cease placing conditions on love, we take a giant step toward learning to love.

So how do we surrender our wants and develop pure love? Even the greatest guru cannot give you love. He can only help by guiding you, offering insights, suggestions, and encouragement. That is why I believe that a total immersion in life is the best classroom for learning to love. Where do I start? An excellent way to begin is by taking loving chances. Consciously choose to participate actively in love and, most important, trust that you are capable of changing.

We cannot change until we believe in our abilities, until we trust in ourselves. But trust alone is not enough: We must also work at it. We cannot simply will our lives to be filled with love. No, we must do the willing *and* the filling.

The overweight person who yearns for a beautiful physique cannot lose weight and develop muscles by desire alone. So it is with love. The desire for love is important, but only through action can love manifest itself. *Love* is a verb, an action word. If we want to love, we must *move* toward love by reaching out to others in love.

Since we live in an imperfect world in which our love is not always returned, it helps to reinforce ourselves in order to continue loving. The lover must often say, "I love because I must, because I will. I love for myself, not for others. I love first for the joy it brings to me, and only secondly for the joy it gives to others. If others return my love and reinforce me, that is good. If they do not, that is also good, for I *will* to love." Lovers must remember that we live for the joy of loving. We hope others do the same thing, but we neither expect nor demand that they do. When they do, we are doubly delighted.

Unfortunately, we sometimes stand in the way of our own love. Our lives are intricate tapestries of relationships. In these relationships, our motivations, desires, needs, and dreams are enmeshed, woven tightly together. We can learn much about ourselves by examining the patterns of our relationships. As we study the tapestries of our lives, it becomes clear that some of the threads block the growth of our love.

In order to enrich our lives with the brilliancy of the colors and threads and patterns of love, we *must* be willing and able to give up certain destructive characteristics — such as the need to be constantly in control, to be always right, to be free of conflict and frustration, to change others for our needs, to be loved by everyone, and to possess.

Even the healthiest among us has some problems relating to others. Whenever two or more individuals move toward one another, even willingly and in love, the processes that bring them together and keep them together are monumentally complex. Balance and security are shaken. Brand-new behaviors are required, or the relationships will fail.

As I noted in concluding my book *Loving Each Other,* there are several strategies we can use to deal with these problems:

We can deny that they exist.

We can acknowledge their existence but avoid doing anything about them.

We can harden ourselves against them and live with them.

We can view them as irreversible and terminate the relationship.

Or we can rise to the challenge of becoming more loving. We can understand that the more we learn about problem solving in relationships, the greater is our ability to love one another.

I hope that you accept the last possibility, for it is my wish that you fill your life with love.

THE DANCE OF THE
WOUNDED HEART

BY *Gabrielle Roth*

*"It may be a natural impulse to love one another, but
how can we love someone if our own heart is stuck? How
do we let someone in if we won't let ourselves out?"*

NOT LONG AGO I was riding in a taxi when the
driver gave me a gift. He told me that in his
native town in Africa, whenever you board
a bus, it is customary to greet everybody onboard. You
greet each person! And if you don't, the other passengers
will think you mad.

The reasoning behind this act is simple — when you get
on, you enter the community of people who are riding the
bus. As a recognition of this community, you greet each
person; it's unheard of that someone would not.

Yet how different we are in the Western world. Such
behavior in a midtown Manhattan bus would be unthink-
able. Here the person greeting each passenger would be
thought absolutely mad.

We crave recognition, yet we don't give it. We want respect, yet we don't take the opportunity to show respect for one another. We're all on the bus, all part of a community, but most often we act as though we're the only one present.

Why is it so difficult for us to love? Love is the natural impulse of the heart. It's the vibe that connects us — to ourselves, to partners, to the community. Certainly we have all been conditioned to love our neighbors as ourselves. Unfortunately, we do just that.

Most modern Western people don't have much love for themselves. The heart is on hold. Waiting to exhale. Waiting to be moved, to be loved, to be seen for who we are. Passively sitting on a volcano. We need to move.

Movement is my master, my teacher. For the past thirty years, I have been falling in love with the dance. I just keep moving. I move alone, move with partners, move in community. Through movement and over time I have come to trust what the body has to say about the heart. It is often a sad, angry, scared message, shoved behind a mask. What it would really like to say when it gets on the bus is "I'm not okay and I hope you're not, either." But nothing is said at all.

It may be a natural impulse to love one another, but how can we love someone if our own heart is stuck? How do we let someone in if we won't let ourselves out?

So many people in our culture have wounded hearts, cutting off our ability to see one another, hear one another clearly. We don't often ask the questions that should be asked: "What does this person need from me right now? What is my offering? What can I give to this other person? How can I give this other person what he or she needs to grow and change, even if it means growing and changing beyond me?"

We have forgotten how to love. We ask, "What can I get out of this relationship? Why aren't you giving me this? How come I'm not getting that?"

We undervalue ourselves. The bottom line is that we don't think we deserve love. This utter lack of self-esteem is paralyzing. If we don't love ourselves, we can't imagine somebody else loving us and yet we want it so badly but we won't let ourselves have it because we might lose it and we already have. Self-negation: You love me? Not possible. You love me? What do you really want? You love me? What's wrong with you?

Some of us rarely lose touch with ourselves but struggle to connect this very same self to another. Some of us resist the group. Fear puts all systems on hold.

That's why I dance. Movement is my practice. Every day I dance the five rhythms: flowing, staccato, chaos, lyrical, and stillness. I call this movement practice the Wave because the rhythms create a wave of energy, the key to unlocking the chambers in my heart. The moment I begin dancing, I know how I feel. My body can't lie.

The message isn't always comforting. There are ghosts trapped in the body, moments of terror, rage, and grief that wander and wail in our physical landscape. Rousting these shadow emotions is a cathartic exercise, not for the weak of heart.

Luckily, the heart is a muscle with soul. Put the psyche into motion, and it heals itself. As soon as your body gets moving, your heart pumps, passions begin to rise. Molecules begin to shift; you know you are alive.

Sometimes being alive is scary. As energy starts to flow,

it sweeps those ghosts through the dancing body like dark clouds in a ferocious sky. The dancing heart goes through the pain. Suffering is part of us, but so is the instinct to express it artistically. You have style, nerve, spontaneity, to spare. In movement, energy is awakened, flowing in and out with your breath.

Movement is my master; I give myself to it totally, all my secrets, all my sorrows, all my fears. I surrender to the dance and let it break my heart a thousand times a day.

I believe that to release the energy which is love, you have to be able to move through the fear that is bonded to the ego, the fear that holds the whole heart in a rigid space or leaves no space for it at all.

I often picture the ego as an extremely efficient Captain Control. Holding the breath. Keeping it all tight and secure. Nothing spontaneous.

Security is a mirage. Life is insecure by its nature. I prefer to practice being insecure. I prefer to practice letting go. I prefer to practice feeling. Fear is a dance. I dance it, it dances me. Movement catalyzes freedom.

Freedom is being in the moment: no past, no future. This innocence heals the wounded heart. Whatever you are holding in your heart, let it go. Perhaps you need to grieve or rage or laugh till you completely fall apart. Do it. To dance is to love your body.

Loving your body opens your heart. If it's not happening in your body, it's not happening. If it's not happening in your body, love is just an abstraction. Love is energy, and energy is motion.

As I practice moving the five rhythms, each rhythm is a teacher. Each takes me into the depths of myself, purifies me, releases all the parts of me; even the parts I deny dance. The rhythms nourish my soul. Each time I nourish my soul, I loosen the ego's hold.

Body, heart, and mind, unified as one — that is the soul. It's not abstract. It's real energy, a real presence that thrives when people are connected — all systems kick in, the psyche is fluid.

My practice is to keep moving. By being responsible for my own energies, I can be responsive to others. Every day I empty out the past. The movements of the Wave are also like the movements of the snake, because I shed the old Gabrielle so that a new one may be born. I have a lot of past to empty out; some parts of it I will be letting go of forever, some parts won't let go of me. I just keep dancing. I dance to give myself permission to be — to be real, honest, raw, vulnerable, and all the things I have been told not to be.

I dance till I am empty. I dance till I am full. My dance is my prayer. I sweat my prayers.

Beginning with Love

BY *John Robbins*

"Give away your love, freely and without expectation. Give it away, and soon your life will be filled with love, and you will have set others on the path of love and peace."

I HAVE BEEN WITH a number of people who were dying and listened to them express regrets over their nearly completed lives. I've heard men say, "I wish I had spent more time with my children, my family, and those that I love," but I've never heard, or even heard of, a single dying person who said, "I wish I'd spent more time with my business or at the office." Being near death offers a person a level of deep sobriety and profound sincerity that most of us do not normally approach. The greatest regrets of almost everyone have to do with not having expressed enough love. The message to us, the living, is clear: love is the single most important aspect of life.

The measure of our lives and the influence that we have on the world and one another is determined by the degree of love and openness in our hearts. If someone is in pain, and if I can allow room in my heart for that pain, then I can be a healing factor in that person's life.

The amount of love and openness in my heart is the basic criterion I use to evaluate myself and my actions. Much of my work, for example, involves social action. I often find myself confronting representatives from the National Cattleman's Association, the National Rifle Association, or other people whose actions seem to me to be very destructive. I find that it's a real test, one of the greatest challenges of social action work, to remain in balance and in a "loving space" with these people, despite the vast differences in our positions and goals. I don't mean this in an egotistic sense of "I'm better than they are and my positions are right, but I'm going to tolerate them." Rather, I'm referring to a genuine sense of acceptance, respect, and love. If we don't keep our hearts open, even to those people whose actions we oppose, we become part of the problem, perpetuating what we are attempting to change: a lack of love.

The importance of infusing every action with love became clear to me many years ago, when I was involved in a peace march in the San Francisco Bay Area. The situation became rather intense when the police were called out and tear gas canisters were fired into the crowd. A man walking beside me actually hit an Oakland police officer over the head with the sign he was carrying, a sign that read PEACE! This action has stuck with me as a metaphor for the contradictory desires with which we often struggle.

The key question is, How can we keep our loving centers in the midst of chaos, confusion, and even insanity? How do we work passionately for peace, for example, without hating our "enemy"? Perhaps part of the solution to these dilemmas comes from recognizing the central importance of love and from acknowledging the fundamental fact that love begins with ourselves. I may not respect or support someone's actions; I may oppose and in some instances even put my life on the line to stop him or her, yet I will not (if I can help it) allow my opposition to anyone's behavior interfere with my relationship to his or her soul.

I always try to remember that there is pain, suffering, and confusion within each of us. I have no doubt that if I knew other people's entire stories, regardless of their positions on certain aspects of life, I would have compassion and understanding for their predicaments and their choices. If I knew what their childhoods were like, the turmoil and difficulties they undoubtedly faced, the pressures that impinge upon their goals and actions, the structures of their psyches and how they feel forced to obey certain impulses, I would most certainly feel compassion and love for them, rather than judging them negatively.

It is particularly hard to bring compassion into our relationships when we feel ourselves to be unlovable. Swimming in a media soup of soap operas, codependent "love" songs, and other forms of popular culture, many of us have learned to moan and complain when we feel that no one loves us. While it's true that feeling unloved is miserable, there is something that we all can do to begin to fill our lives with love. And that something is simply to give our love to others. We can always do that, because love isn't something that we "get" or "find." Rather, it is something that we create within ourselves and give to others.

I never really felt a part of my family while I was growing up. I felt alienated. I didn't know how to love my sisters and my parents. Like most parents, mine wanted me to conform to their expectations, to follow the script that they had in mind for my life. I would have done so in order to please them, but I couldn't, because what they wanted for me was contrary to my inner callings and my destiny. This difference made them unhappy with me and contributed to quite a bit of pain in my family. I often felt like a total failure when I could not please my parents.

However, early on I realized that I could please my cat by petting her. When she purred and loved me back, I realized that my love made a difference to this beautiful animal; and this love meant a lot to me. I discovered that when I found a place to pour out my love, I felt better. I was happiest when I was loving her, petting her, talking to her, and looking after her needs.

As an adult, I find it thrilling to look at a bird or a deer or a cow and realize that the same life force that runs through me, and through the rest of us, also runs through that animal. I can feel a powerful connectedness that lies at the heart of love and spirituality. Unfortunately, although animals can be receptive to our love, our society tends to treat them as commodities. In factory farms, for example, the cruelty inflicted upon the animals is almost indescribably severe. I don't tell people that they should be vegetarians or where they should draw their lines. I do, however, want them to know about this suffering so that they can make their own choices. It's helpful to ask, "What does my life stand for?" so we do not find ourselves supporting something that violates our essential values.

Sadly, many of us are estranged from ourselves, from one another, and from nature. Half of all marriages end in divorce, families are scattered across the country, children grow up shuttling back and forth between parents and stepsiblings. During times like these, we can benefit from remembering that the key to love is to love what is available, rather than to reserve all our love for one person, idea, or thing. Instead of waiting for perfection or for the ideal, and instead of closing our hearts to those with whom we disagree, we can love everyone we come into contact with. We can even act loving toward people we do not know and have never met.

There are several toll bridges in the Bay Area, where I live. Not too long ago, some people began paying the tolls of the cars immediately behind them as "random act of kindness." The drivers of these "cars behind" were undoubtedly surprised and delighted to be told that "your toll has been paid by the car ahead of you." This is an example of a spontaneous gift, one given without expectations of or demands for anything in return. I did this for a while, then had an unusual insight. Why not perform a random act of kindness for someone I could see and briefly meet? Such people were right in front of me breathing auto exhaust all day long while collecting tolls from countless cars. So I began giving "tips" to the toll takers. I'd say, "Keep the change," smiling as I drove off. These moments of personal contact were even more valuable to me than the more impersonal act of paying the toll for the car behind me.

There is a little of Donald Trump and a little of Mother Teresa in each of us. Part of us wants to acquire and rule, while another part of us yearns to be of service to others, to love, care for, nurture, and protect. A great way to do so, while simultaneously feeling an integral part of the world, is simply to love others: your friends, your neighbors, your relatives, and even your "opponents." Give away your love, freely and without expectation. Give it away, and soon your life will be filled with love, and you will have set others on the path of love and peace.

Breathing In Love

by *Jean Shinoda Bolen, M.D.*

"I think people don't place a high enough value on how much they are nurtured by doing whatever it is that totally absorbs them. Whenever people are totally caught up in what they are doing — their passion — a timeless quality exists in which they are expressing the real essence of their authentic self. And this genuine essence, this authentic self, thereby helps their inner love grow."

LOVE IS AN ENERGY that surrounds us, an energy to which we give particular form through an open heart. It logically follows that the more we open our heart, the more our lives are filled with love; the more love we give away, the more we become filled with it.

On a physiological level, our bodies function best if we breathe deeply and fill our lungs with oxygen. However, unlike the body, where the breathing mechanism normally happens whether we want it to or not, we must consciously fill our heart and our lives with love in order to live lives rich in love and its blessings. We need to take love in and send it back out again. The more we engage in this cycle, the healthier we become and the more our lives are filled with love. Just as the physical heart fills and empties almost one hundred times a minute, the "invisible heart" needs to do the same thing. It needs to keep moving— love in, love out, giving, receiving. Unlike the physical heart, which operates instinctively, the soul heart takes in and gives out as a choice. We must choose to fill our heart with love from the people in our lives and from the love that exists in nature and the universe. To breathe in love, to receive it, we need to see the beauty and open our heart to it. We need to meditate on what is peaceful. Once we are "filled up" in this way, we once again have an abundance of love to send out into the world.

We give our love to the world from that place of soul where we share the inner side of ourselves with others. We have a choice about how we show our soul place. If a soul is filled with love, a soul place is very different from one that is filled with obsession, anger, or resentment. If the psyche is filled with these negative feelings, there is no room for love to move through us. It is the equivalent of a lung that has emphysema or a physical body that is disabled and hasn't learned to function optimally.

We come into the world ready to receive and learn about love, and to give it back. A baby is born into the world as a lovable, vulnerable bundle, capable of evoking love and actually needing it to physically grow. Babies who aren't loved die, even if all their physical needs are taken care of. Without touch, smiles, and comforting affection, they fail to thrive, they stop growing, and they eventually die of depression. It's as if our very matter, our cells, require a certain amount of love even to grow on a physical level. As adults, we no longer need love to grow physically; nevertheless, it remains an essential nutrient for the soul.

We are born into this world wanting most of all to be loved. Babies who come into a healthy environment bring joy just by being born. When we are babies, the world smiles at us and we smile back. We have the sense of being in a friendly universe that loves us. That feeling is what we all hope for, but it doesn't always happen. Sometimes we are either denied love or loved so conditionally that we have to suppress entire parts of ourselves to be acceptable. Then the natural order, the way things are supposed to be, is upset. A common response to feeling unloved is to begin using defensive maneuvers. People who feel unloved feel they must accumulate and use power to protect themselves. This obsessive interest in power limits faith and eventually limits accomplishments. When you are bound up by feeling conditionally accepted or trapped in co-dependent types of behavior so that others value you, your interactions with the world no longer have to do with love but are motivated by the intense desire to feel accepted.

So much of what brings people into consultation offices, both psychological as well as medical, has to do with their unhappiness: feeling as if they, as individuals, don't matter. A self-negating internalized critic, a harsh judge, has taken over. This critic assumes that the person will be what someone else expects, rather than being his or her own true self. There is a discrepancy between the self the person really is — spontaneous, instinctive, and natural — and who he or she presents to the world. This dichotomy creates an enormous amount of unhappiness that eventually manifests itself in physical and psychological symptoms. I believe that at the root of this problem is a lack of that essential nutrient, love.

I think there is some kind of perception, deep within us, that knows whether there is love in the environment or not. I don't think we are consciously aware of it, any more than we are consciously aware of the percentage of oxygen in a polluted environment. But at some instinctive level, just as we know whether we are breathing in good air or not, we know whether there is love around us. This awareness is important, because when the love gauge reads "low," we can consciously choose to bring love back into our environment through our conscious choices.

Many years ago I made a kind of rule for myself that I wouldn't agree to do anything unless it was fun and meaningful. Fun for me has to do with the quality of the people involved, their openheartedness. If they are fun to be with, then I can be myself and laugh and, if necessary, cry. I can be honest, and there is no need to put on a false face. I love Anne Morrow Lindbergh's words that being insincere is the hardest work there is. So whenever I have the choice, I ask myself, "Is it fun? Is it meaningful?" If the love energy will flow naturally and fully, then I can go ahead. In the same way that we can choose to bring in love, we also have to know when to move away from those situations that take love out of our lives. If you sense that someone is doing something out of unlovingness, and you know you'll be affected by it, there is a real need to say no. In order to fill our lives with love, we must learn to think and act selectively.

I think people don't place a high enough value on how much they are nurtured by doing whatever it is that totally absorbs them. Whenever people are totally caught up in what they are doing — their passion — a timeless quality exists in which they are expressing the real essence of their authentic self. And this genuine essence, this authentic self, thereby helps their inner love grow. The activity could be anything: doing brain surgery, straightening up a room, or painting a picture. Whatever it is, if it makes their heart happy, they are extending who they truly are, not only into what they are doing but into the love that flows through the universe. What love could be greater than giving our world the gift of our authentic selves?

Being Love

BY *Ram Dass*

"Remember, we are all affecting the world every moment, whether we mean to or not. Our actions and states of mind matter, because we're so deeply interconnected with one another. Working on our own consciousness is the most important thing that we are doing at any moment, and being love is the supreme creative act."

THE MOST IMPORTANT aspect of love is not in the giving or the receiving: it's in the being. When I need love from others, or need to give love to others, I'm caught in an unstable situation. *Being* in love, rather than giving or taking love, is the only thing that provides stability. Being in love means seeing the Beloved all around me.

I'm not interested in becoming a "lover." I'm interested only in being love. In our culture we think of love as a relational thing: "I love you" and "you are my lover." But while the ego is built around relationship, the soul is not. It wants only to *be* love. It's a true joy, for example, to turn someone whom you don't initially like into the Beloved. One way I practice doing so is by placing a photograph of a politician with whom I intensely disagree on my *puja* table — my altar. Each morning when I wake up, I say good morning to the Buddha, to my guru, and to the other holy beings there. But I find it's with a different spirit that I say, "Hello, Mr. Politician." I know it sounds like a funny thing to do, but it reminds me of how far I have to go to see the Beloved in everybody. Mother Teresa has described this as "seeing Christ in all his distressing disguises." When I realized that Mother Teresa was actually involved in an intimate love affair with each and every one of the poor and the lepers she was picking up from the gutters in India, I thought to myself, "That's the way to play the game of love." And that's what I've been training myself to do for the past quarter century: to see and be with the Beloved everywhere.

One of the interesting aspects of seeing the Beloved in this way is that it doesn't require the other person to see him- or herself as the Beloved. All that's necessary is that I focus my own consciousness properly. It's interesting to notice, though, how warmly people respond to being seen as the Beloved, even if they don't know what's happening. (Of course, all this assumes that your feelings are genuine and that you aren't compelled to act on them or to lay any sort of trip on the other person. The idea is simply to live and breathe among the Beloved.)

The way I work at seeing others (like the politician) as the Beloved is to remind myself, "This is another soul, just like me, who has taken a complicated incarnation, just as I have. I don't want to be in his incarnation any more than he wants to be in mine. But since I want to rest in my soul and not in my ego, I would like to give everybody else the opportunity to do the same."

If I can see the soul that happens to have incarnated into a person that I don't care for, then my consciousness becomes an environment in which he or she is free to come up for air if he or she wants to. That person can do so because I'm not trying to keep him or her locked into being the person he or she has become. It's liberating to resist another person politically, yet still see him or her as another soul. That's what Krishna meant when he said, "I'm not going to fight, because they are all my cousins on the other side." We may disagree with one another in our current incarnation, but we are all souls.

A story I have told many times reinforces this point. Some years ago I put out a set of records called *Love, Serve, Remember*. The records — which had music, readings from the Gospel of John, and all kinds of neat things — came in an album with a beautiful booklet with text and pictures. It was a wonderful package, and we sold it by mail order for about $4.50.

I showed the album to my father. Dad was a wealthy Boston lawyer — a conservative Republican, a capitalist, and, at the time, the president of a railroad. He looked over the album and said, "Great job here! But, gee, you know — four and a half dollars? You could probably sell this for ten dollars — fifteen dollars, even!"

I said, "Yeah, I know."

"Would fewer people buy it if it were more expensive?" he asked.

"No," I replied. "Probably the same number would buy it."

"Well, I don't understand you," he pressed on. "You could sell it for ten, and you're selling it for four-fifty? What's wrong, are you against capitalism or something?"

I tried to figure out how to explain to him how our approaches differed. I said, "Dad, didn't you just try a law case for Uncle Henry?"

"Yeah," he replied, "and it was a damned tough case. I spent a lot of time in the law library."

I asked, "Did you win the case?" And he answered, "Yeah, I won it."

Now, my father was a very successful attorney, and he charged fees that were commensurate with his reputation. So I continued. "Well, I'll bet you charged him an arm and a leg for that one!"

Dad was indignant at the suggestion. "What, are you out of your mind? That's Uncle Henry—I couldn't charge him!"

"Well, that's my problem," I said. "If you find anyone who isn't Uncle Henry, I'll rip them off."

The point I was trying to make is that when you see the Beloved all around you, everyone is family and everywhere is love. When I allow myself to really see the beauty of another being, to see the inherent beauty of a soul manifesting itself, I feel a quality of love in that being's presence. It doesn't matter what we're doing. We could be talking about our cats because we happen to be picking out cat food in the supermarket, or we could simply be passing each other on the sidewalk. When we are being love, we extend outward an environment that allows others to act in different, more loving and peaceful ways than they are used to behaving. Not only does it allow them to be more loving, it encourages them to be so.

In 1969 I was giving a series of lectures in New York

City. Every night, taking the bus up Third Avenue, I got the same extraordinary bus driver. Every night it was rush hour in one of the busiest cities in the world, but he had a warm word and a caring presence for each person who got on the bus. He drove as if he were sculling a boat down a river, flowing through the traffic rather than resisting it. Everyone who got on that bus was less likely to kick the dog that evening or to be otherwise hostile and unloving, because of the loving space that driver had created. Yet all he was doing was driving his bus. He wasn't a therapist or a great spiritual teacher. He was simply being love.

Remember, we are all affecting the world every moment, whether we mean to or not. Our actions and states of mind matter, because we're so deeply interconnected with one another. Working on our own consciousness is the most important thing that we are doing at any moment, and being love is the supreme creative act.

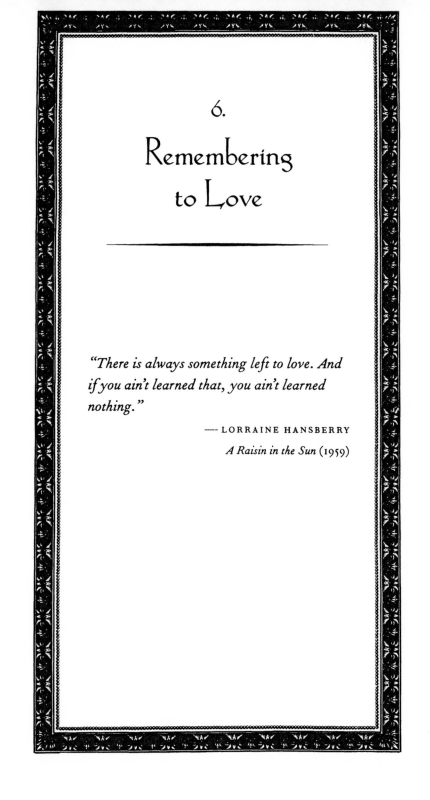

6.

Remembering
to Love

"There is always something left to love. And if you ain't learned that, you ain't learned nothing."

—LORRAINE HANSBERRY

A Raisin in the Sun (1959)

HEART LESSONS

BY *Bernie Siegel, M.D.*

"So I began to stop and think when somebody entered the room: If I love this person, how would I behave toward him or her? And, of course, what I found was that the more I acted this way, the more loving and sensitive I became. And the other people are changed by simply being loved; it really becomes easier to love them. With this basic approach, over time I changed myself, my body, my state of health, my relationships, and many other aspects of my life."

THIS IS THE ESSENCE of how I help myself remain aware of my feelings: I write a poem whenever something moves me. This one came after watching a story on television about Lassie.

> I love Lassie, Lassie loves me.
> Lassie is love.
> A dog, a dog, a dog teaches love.
> I'm going to set my sights on becoming a dog.
> I have a role model now.

So that's how I manage. Whenever I wonder how to be more loving, I behave as if I were Lassie.

Love is so important. When we're in pain, if someone is there for us, loving us, we receive the greatest gift in the world and we ultimately hurt a lot less. I hope that someday we shall reach a point where it is normal for people to love well and fully. It's certainly not that we don't have enough information about how to love, but many of us don't have the ability, because we weren't loved ourselves. The best way around this problem is to practice and rehearse loving behavior daily.

Years ago I asked the anthropologist Ashley Montagu how I could be a more loving human being. I said, "For example, if my mother-in-law moves into my house and I want to have a better relationship with her, be more loving with her, what can I do?" And he said, "When your mother-in-law comes in the room, behave as if you love her." I thought this advice sounded superficial, but then I realized that I really wanted to achieve this mindset. I wasn't trying to fool my mother-in-law or my wife or my children or anyone else. I only want to love them more. So I began to stop and think when somebody entered the room: If I love this person, how would I behave toward him or her? And, of course, what I found was that the more I acted this way, the more loving and sensitive I became. And the other people are changed by simply being loved; it really becomes easier to love them. With this basic approach, over time I changed myself, my body, my state of health, my relationships, and many other aspects of my life.

Learning to love more effectively merely involves performing and practicing like a movie star or an athlete. When someone says to actors or athletes, "Oh, you're such a lucky person to be born with this skill," they look at the person as if to say, "Wait a minute, I am a wonderful performer or athlete, not because I was born with this skill, but because I spent a lot of time practicing and rehearsing and working my way up." So becoming a lover works exactly the same way — rehearsing and practicing. Find role models. A person could say, "What would the Buddha or Jesus do in this situation? Or Moses, Confucius, Gandhi, the Dalai Lama, Mother Teresa, Martin Luther King, Jr.?" Or just imagine how a loving mother would act. And if that's too hard, then you can always go back to "What would Lassie do?" A dog will lick your face, even if you ignore it. Unless repeatedly abused, a dog will lick your face, even when a vet has amputated a limb or is about to put it to death. It simply doesn't hold on to hostility. It is here to love, be loved, and along the way teach us a few things.

All the world's a theater, and we can choose how to act. We're given a lifetime to practice and can become as good as we want to be. But we must remember that we cannot perform well all the time. Therefore, we need to be forgiving of ourselves and others, recognizing that we're doing the best we can at any moment.

As a physician, I have found that being good at loving has nothing to do with physical health. There are plenty of wonderful lovers out there who are missing parts of their bodies or the ability to move. I call these "the healthy people," but it has nothing to do with the state of their bodies or their physical health. Sometimes, in fact, it takes the threat of death for people to pay attention to love and to make it a priority. Our mortality can be a great teacher.

It's hard for people who don't know how to play, who've lost that childlike quality, to be lovers because

they are more likely to be hostile. Love and play go together. People who have studied pathological killers say
that many of them just don't know how to play. They can't
kid around. Everything is serious.

Laughter brings out the child in everybody. It diffuses
much of the fear and resentment people have of one another, making it easier to be loving. Just look at your baby
picture and you'll know how easy it is to love that child.
Now look in the mirror. Do you have the same feelings?
Why not?

To encourage love at the hospital (this can also be done
in any office), I give out rainbow pins with people's names
that say, "You make a difference." If I saw people acting in
a loving way, I would get their names and give them pins
and thank them. Just think, if everybody who was dedicated to love wore a symbol, you would behave differently
toward them when you saw them.

I was lucky to be brought up loved. Not that everything
I did was liked, but I knew that I was loved — and knowing this gave me the ability and freedom to be who I
wanted to be. Because I had my parents' support, I didn't
need everybody else's approval and I could be loving and
free. The benefit of this kind of support is that when you
want to be different, you can, because you know you will
always be accepted. When I married, I always knew that I
could come home to a loving person who accepted me. So,
if I were a little bizarre, crazy, or whatever, I had a place to
go. Even when disturbing things happened to me, I knew I
could go home, where I was still number one.

Sadly, others are not so fortunate. People who have not
been loved as children are often in a great deal of pain,
even if they do not show it outwardly. We need to communicate about the pain we suffer and listen to one another in

order to heal. We can't assume that everyone thinks or feels like we do.

I suggest that we have an American Society for the Prevention of Cruelty to Humans, like the ASPCA. Basically, I want people to love themselves and others as they would a pet. Some people feed themselves things they would never feed their pets. They'll take drugs they wouldn't give their pets. People exercise their pets, while they themselves just sit around. They hug their pets but not their own families. People need to be as kind to themselves as they are to their pets. We have the information but not the inspiration.

In my practice, I've often seen that people wouldn't take the necessary steps to stay healthy. I learned that for most people wellness becomes a spiritual journey. So in trying to inspire people, I ask them, "Why are you here? Why were you born? Why is the world the way it is? What is all this about?" And my answer is that we're here to learn to love more fully, to be God or angels in disguise for one another, to show our love, to show our compassion, to be active in creation. That is the reason and the meaning behind our lives. Each of us has a choice about how to love the world in our unique way.

Wherever I lecture, I hear people complaining about how other people act at work or at home. They often let their irritations ruin their lives. To have a happy life, we have to practice loving people, including their imperfections, which means learning and practicing tolerance and compassion. If you are here for a limited time, would you rather spend it being irritated or being loving?

Here's a story about how I once handled a disagreement with my wife, Bobbie. The handles broke off some cups because of the way I put them in the dishwasher. My wife wanted to throw them out. I didn't. I thought they were still useful. So I just put the cups in a bag to hide them and prevent divorce proceedings. I took them to our vacation house where my wife wouldn't see them as often. One morning while we were on Cape Cod, I went out jogging as usual with a plastic bag to pick up either things that God leaves me along the way or recyclables. I was running along and saw a cup with a broken handle lying in the road. I knew it was a message from God. So I ran over, picked it up, turned it over, and saw a drawing of two fat elephants hugging under mistletoe. Inscribed on the cup was "I love you just the way you are." I brought the cup home and showed it to Bobbie. Now the cup sits on a shelf in our house, reminding us every day of the real message of life. (The other cups are now accepted and used by my wife.)

When you're a lover, you don't destroy — whether it's nature, society, or an individual. Children who have plants and animals learn to care and nurture a reverence for life.

At any given time, our five children used to have up to a hundred creatures in our home, including three dozen turtles in kiddy pools, lizards, dogs, skunks, and crickets. I tried to teach my kids that if they had a life in their hands, they cared for it and eventually became an expert in its care. I think a child brought up this way is going to be a lot different as an adult from one who learns that suffering is meaningless and it's okay to kill a neighbor or torture animals or that a neighbor isn't the right color, shape, or whatever. As our son Jeff said, "The animals get along because they're all the same color inside." So are we.

I suggest that people keep a journal or write a poem every day, like the one I wrote about Lassie. It helps them get in touch with all aspects of life, including the painful ones. It's important to write not only about the tough stuff, which we tend to remember, but also about the good and funny events. If people can see the humor in a tense situation, then they can laugh and diffuse the anger.

It's great when parents can act childlike, because their kids notice and then feel free to behave that way. Making others laugh is such a loving act, because if love didn't exist between people, they wouldn't be interested in laughing or in making another person laugh. Perhaps if we can all become a little less serious, laugh more often, and act more loving toward ourselves and others, we can live in a more loving world and, as this book suggests, we can all fill our lives with love.

THE ATMOSPHERE
OF LOVE

BY *Daphne Rose Kingma*

"We need to change our vision of love to realize that we live in a universe created and sustained by love and that we're able to experience this love in every venue in our lives — in our language, in our sexuality, in our friendships, in our work, in our service, in our suffering, in our transformation, in our living, and in our dying."

I REMEMBER A CERTAIN period in my life when, to my great joy and amazement, I discovered that my life was filled with love. As a child I had observed people in the small scenes of their relationships — at church, at the park, waiting for the trolley — and I remember thinking, "Oh, isn't that beautiful, isn't that wonderful, look at how they're talking with one another, look how they're holding hands, how they're comforting one another." This was very moving to me. And then at some point in my life I suddenly realized that I too was living that experience.

We tend to think that love is going to be the exception in our lives, that if we're really, really lucky we're going to have an experience of love, we're going to fall in love, or we're going to have a lover or a great friend. But the truth is that love is really the ground of our being. It's the atmosphere in which we experience everything we undertake: it's everything we are, it's every person we encounter. We need to change our vision of love to realize that we live in a universe created and sustained by love and that we're able to experience this love in every venue in our lives — in our language, in our sexuality, in our friendships, in our work, in our service, in our suffering, in our transformation, in our living, and in our dying.

Unhappily, it's part of the human mental structure to create an idea — literally an idea — that love is a thing apart from us, a thing we can isolate as a particular experience. We need to change this view, move it from the foreground to the background. We need to take love from the particular to the universal. This, above all, is what can bring more love into our lives.

There are many ways to acknowledge that love is not a thing apart, that it is, in fact, a part of everything we do, think, and feel. Some people say affirmations; some put their energies into looking for someone with whom to share their lives. But no matter how we go about coming into the love that is always there for us, we all need to proceed with two attitudes: intention and surrender. We all have masculine and feminine energies: intention is the masculine; surrender, the feminine. And it's a paradoxical combination of those energies that brings love into our lives. This means that love is both something we have to consciously pursue (proceeding with intent) and something that we must simply let happen (or surrender to). So, for example, we may take action by saying, "I'm now looking for a partner to love" or "I'm going to make a list of every beautiful thing that happens to me so that I'm aware that every day I'm being loved in some form or another." Or we may surrender, saying, "I'm going to be available to the unexpected love that is being offered to me moment by moment," whether it comes from the stranger who pays you a compliment or from the workmen who are improving your house, or whether it's a breathtaking experience with your beloved in a moment of exquisite intimacy in a sexual encounter, in a moment of shared grief, in a moment of expressed vulnerability. We need to be both open to receive and also actively and consciously seeking to receive. If you approach life this way, then love becomes not an exception in your life, but the very context in which you experience life.

There are many ways we take love for granted, things that happen every day and are so much a part of our lives that instead of seeing them as love, we treat them as invisible. To see them and receive them all as gifts of love, we need to move beyond the very particular, finite, romantic view of love and into the infinite frame. Now, of course, romantic love is absolutely delicious, embracing as it does the "falling in love" part where there is sexual attraction and a dream of the future. But if we're stuck thinking that's the only form that love can take, without it we'll feel we're not experiencing love at all.

I believe that we have an opportunity, in this final decade of the century, to expand and blossom our love consciousness, to change our definition of love, and to realize that love is available to us in every moment in the most surprising forms. I'll give you an example: I was in Hawaii a few weeks ago. I was very weary, from a vast fire that happened to my house. I was lying on the beach, incredibly exhausted. I didn't want to talk to a living soul.

And a little girl came up to me with a pinwheel and said, "Can I sing you a song?" She sang a beautiful little song about friendship. The last line was "So I'm singing you this song and I want to be your friend, will you be my friend, too?" It was an absolutely exquisite gift. I will never see her again, I don't know her name, but we had an experience of deep connectedness and true love in that moment on the beach. There are hundreds of these moments in life that are so tiny that they don't register on this chart that we've all built about what love is. We think love has to look a certain way, have a certain outcome. But we're constantly gifted with such moments, experiences that are just breathtaking in their purity and their absolutely consecrated perfection.

When we zero in on a narrow definition of love, we lose sight of all the love we are actually receiving and our lives lack a sense of richness, even though we are constantly being blessed with the riches of love. Instead of feeling immersed in love, we're always one step removed from it, sort of waiting for it to happen to us. Yet love is really the atmosphere; it's all around us. Recently I had a lot of workmen here, repairing the damage from the fire. And I felt that they were blessing me, loving me through their craftsmanship and their kindness and their willingness to be a part of this restoration and renewal of my life. They were in good spirits and they all did their work so beautifully; this was an experience of love. They were giving their gift, and I was able to love them by receiving it and by participating in their lives and their livelihood by paying them.

These are all transactions of love, although we don't tend to think of them this way. But this is how love is the very atmosphere that we live in. It's like the air. If we didn't have air, we would not be able to sustain our lives.

And love, like the air, is a continuous, constant, life-giving presence that sustains us all, literally, in ways that we don't even know and can't comprehend.

There is an incredibly beautiful elegance in all of our interactions with people and nature. In my own life, recently I have been asking for many transformations because an era of my life is ending. I intuitively sensed that I was ready to take on another chapter of my life. And this new beginning was given to me in the form of a wandering troubled person who set my house on fire. In a sense, this person, whom I didn't even know, gave me the gift of liberation and transformation. I won't ever see him or know him, like the little girl at the beach, but on a soul level, I want to say thank you. Thank you for being the suffering person whose action set me free.

I think that we're all being asked, in a very profound way at this time in history, to reconnect with the truth that love is the very atmosphere in which we live. We are being invited to overcome the mechanistic relationship to love that has created the tremendous catastrophe that we're perpetrating on the planet. As the world was conceived, there was an interrelationship between human creatures and animals and plants and trees that was perfectly balanced. This was a relationship of love.

Then we got the idea that we needed to make a distinction between "mine" and "yours," "ours" and "theirs"; we entered into that atmosphere of love in a very controlling and divisive way, which robbed us of our understanding of the world, that it is part of an infinite universe we can't even begin to comprehend, a universe that is the embodiment and the enactment of infinite love. We're living out our little part of it, and we're trying to decide what it means. But we have a very limited perspective, so we say,

"Well, this can't be love because it doesn't feel like my idea of love." But the truth is, if we changed our idea of love, we would suddenly comprehend it. We've asked love to fit our definitions instead of being open for love to teach us what it is.

I believe there are two things that all of us can do on a very simple level to have a greater experience of love: express love and receive it. We have thousands of opportunities every day to express love — with our bodies; with our language; with our choices; with our relationships to our possessions, to our children, to the other people we love, and to strangers on the street. If we start expressing the truth of our connection to other people, we will begin to feel more love, to feel that the world is a more harmonious place, that we belong in it and that it is a gracious, genteel, compassionate environment. We can say to the stranger or the friend, "You are beautiful" or "I see that you are suffering and I reach out my hand to you" or "You're blessing me with your wisdom" or "You're kind" or "Your words are touching." Conversely, when they are offered to us we can receive all these minute, beautiful gifts, taking them into the infinite brilliance of our hearts and minds and be transformed by them. For there *are* incredible gifts, every day. Just being alive is a gift. Just waking up is a gift. You may be doing some awful chores on this particular day, but it's a beautiful day: you're alive, you're here.

It's so easy to let all these gifts go unnoticed and unmentioned. We need to acknowledge them openly — for the world and for ourselves, because when we don't openly express ourselves about them, it's not just that the other person doesn't get the compliment, it's that we ourselves are not reminded that life is generous and good and that we are constantly in the presence of love. Conversely, every time we do speak up about them, love becomes part of our body of memory. I use the expression *body of memory* because it is in our bodies that we carry these memories of an infinity of love experiences that I believe reach back even beyond this lifetime. Every time we do acknowledge these love moments, on a molecular, cellular level, our bodies are being reminded that life is graceful and gracious. And that becomes our world. We allow the flow of love to come in; we know we're in a sea of love, a bath of love, an atmosphere of love that's constantly accessible if only we are willing to receive it. And when we receive it, we can say to ourselves, "Thank you, I've been touched, honored, recognized" — and the true miracle of our being here in life has been momentarily celebrated and acknowledged.

Sharing love takes many forms: words and gestures and passion and things we create such as art and music and literature, film, and theater. In the world of love there is a constant dialogue and choreography of expression and reception. There is also the internal personal stance that says, "I'm going to be very still and know that everything is working beautifully; my life is, at every second, meaningful and rich beyond bounds." To come to this place, all we really have to do is understand that love is the atmosphere, the very air we breathe. Then we can give love and receive it — breathe out, breathe in — and love will always fill our lives.

LOVE AND LETTING BE

BY *John Welwood, Ph.D.*

"To love a person for who he or she is — apart from our desires and projections — calls on us to wake up from our dreams and fantasies. It brings us up against the obstacles to love — all the places where we are tight or closed down inside. If you are willing to work with these obstacles, you start to open up in new ways and become more fully engaged."

T O TRULY LOVE people, we must first be able to let them be — let them be who they are, not who we would like them to be. True love involves loving people's *being*, not just their personality, their looks, or what they do for you. To do so requires a certain kind of discernment, or awareness, of who a person really is. True love never tries to tell someone who or what he or she should be. The same is true for loving yourself. You have to learn to see who you really are, behind all your thoughts and images about who you are.

Though love is often shrouded in projection and imagination, it is really about truth. Truly loving calls on us to wake up and see things as they actually are, see the truth about ourselves and about the ones we love.

Love is much more than showering someone with positive feelings. Many parents "drown" a child in "love," without seeing who the child really is. They see their *version* of the child, and love that image. This happens between lovers as well: we may love our image of the other, or our image of ourselves when we are with that person.

How to see the truth? It helps to take some time out of our busy lives every day to tune in, through meditation or just sitting quietly, to connect with who we really are, underneath our personality, underneath our mind, underneath our thoughts, emotions, and plans — everything we know or think about ourselves. Simply being present, being ourselves, feeling and contacting who we are, in a quiet, nameless way. It's also good to do this with others, to practice opening ourselves to them just as they are, without trying to make them fit into some agenda we might have.

Tuning in to who another person really is — as opposed to who you would *like* him or her to be — is very challenging. It brings us up against obstacles: our hopes, fears, and needs, or our desire to control ourselves and everything in our surroundings. Love without awareness easily becomes distorted. It can become a tool for controlling others and can be given as a reward or withheld as a punishment for behavior that's deemed either "good" or "bad."

But true love is never an instrument of control. It involves letting someone be. This freedom is not something passive. Instead, it involves active support and encouragement. You want someone you love to flourish in his or her own particular way, so you give this person the space to do just that. This is true nourishment. It's the opposite of "smothering with love." Those who smother with love are not giving the loved one space to be who he or she is — they're trying to make the person an extension of themselves.

To love a person for who he or she is — apart from our desires and projections — calls on us to wake up from our dreams and fantasies. It brings us up against the obstacles to love — all the places where we are tight or closed down inside. If you are willing to work with these obstacles, you start to open up in new ways and become more fully engaged. Your love is put to the test. You go through a baptism of fire and may even wonder, "Do I really have what it takes to love someone, or even love myself?" But when love is aligned with the truth, existing in the service of the truth, then it eventually conquers all — all the obstacles to being who we really are. We come out of that fire more real, more open, and truly loving.

My work as a psychotherapist is not about "helping" my clients or "fixing" them, or giving them answers or advice. It's mostly about providing a space in which they can let go of the chains that keep them from being who they are. I try to provide an open space of truth and inquiry that's full of encouragement for them to be themselves. I don't have any particular agenda and don't suggest that my clients have an agenda for themselves. I just give them the opportunity to look at what's going on, feel what they feel, open themselves to their experiences, and develop some insight into their situations. Once they can respond to this invitation, the rest of the process almost happens on its own.

This kind of being-with does not require a "gushy" kind of love, but something more like compassion. It's warm, it's inviting, and it allows a person to unfold, like a flower. In more than twenty years as a therapist, I've found that this is the most powerful thing in terms of helping someone. This compassion doesn't involve a lot of instruction. It just provides a space, a permission, an encouragement, a support, and a presence. In that kind of space, people can begin to find their own way and blossom.

This is what we all really want, what our heart wants, what our soul wants — this space to just be. This is also what we wanted from our parents. We wanted them to be *present* with us. We wanted them to see who we really were. That kind of presence and support is the most valuable thing you can give a child. But instead, what many parents give their children is the message "We love you when you're like this, and we're critical of you when you're like that." That kind of conditional love is a form of control, because it is used as a reward or punishment. So we grew up learning to do the things we were rewarded for. And that became a prison.

You can continue to live in the prison that you and your parents constructed together, doing things so that you'll get the rewards of "love." But this is like being a rat in a cage, pressing the bar to get food. You keep pressing that bar, trying to get the same empty kind of rewards and reinforcement from other people that you got from your parents, because you didn't get the real thing — genuine recognition and acceptance.

But the truth is that you are valuable and beautiful just as you are. Your very nature *is* beauty; *is* value; *is* love; *is* presence, openness, and clarity; *is* richness, power, and generosity. These qualities are already who you are. Once you recognize this about yourself and about others, you are able to give and receive love freely.

When the obstacles to love arise, and inevitably they will, it's important to open yourself to seeing and feeling what is coming up, to develop a willingness to inquire into what is happening, and to enlarge a capacity to let yourself have your feelings, whatever they may be. Every time you try to block or suppress some feeling or perception, you actually disconnect from yourself. And if you are not connected with yourself, it's impossible to truly connect with others.

I try to meditate every day. I find that it helps me sharpen my awareness and perception. This is very important. It is also helpful to set aside time to pay attention to my feelings, to inquire into them, and to let myself hear what they are trying to tell me. My wife, Jennifer, and I also set aside special time for what we call "truth telling." We each try to say what we're going through and then really try to hear what the other has to say. Often it's difficult to hear the other person's truth, but we try to give each other this kind of space and presence, which has been very helpful to us. What is most simple (and difficult) is just to reveal your experience to someone and to hear and understand what it's like for the other person as well. When my wife and I reach the point where we can simply hear and understand how the other feels, we feel loving again, even when struggling with a very difficult issue. Then, even if we still have not reached agreement about what we are discussing, we can usually find a way to work it out.

Love and awareness *are* our essential nature. They are always already present, so it's a question of being able to tune into that and clear away the obstacles, which are mostly mental. Our habitual thought forms are like clouds in the sky. The vast sky of love and awareness is always open and always calling to us, even though the clouds may sometimes block it. The key is to tune in to this vast sky behind the clouds and to know that it's our true nature. The clouds evaporate when we bring the warmth of our hearts to bear on them. Awareness and compassion for ourselves and others chases away those clouds and eventually allows us to reconnect with our true nature — which is love, caring, openness, and warmth.

Living from the Heart

by *Helen Hunt, M.A.*

"Empathy cannot happen from the mind. It is a pure heart function. Often it is the proverbial breaking of the heart that ushers in the powerful onset of empathy. Though pain may crack the heart open — leaving us raw — rather than taking something away from us, it offers us a chance to be present to our own life process, to feel the heart stirrings — even though there is pain."

T HE CAPACITY TO LOVE, to develop in heart and empathy, is fundamental to our worldwide survival. We are inherently connected with all other beings on this planet. Within nature, we are all interrelated, inexplicably linked together to form the miraculous whole called earth. This awareness enables us to fulfill our destinies within the human collective — while contributing our uniqueness to the healing of the world.

One of the most common dis-eases in our society is the feeling of isolation. People go into therapy feeling alone.

They not only feel isolated but feel alone in this feeling of isolation. This isolation manifests itself in so many ways, from the inability to form or stay in a relationship, to the experience of "being outside looking in," "cut off," "left out" wherever we go. The sense of isolation is paralyzing to the spirit. If people are convinced that they are alone and unapproachable, their heart is cut off from others. They cannot engage with others or with life, for they have ceased to engage with their own heart-self. The joy and fulfillment of sharing love seems forever unattainable.

Love is the experience of a constant opening to self and others — the willingness to receive and send the joy of a shared life, a shared moment. It is deeply gratifying on a personal level to feel cherished and to be able to cherish someone. On a more abstract level, this shared love is the way to feel a part of the human family.

Loving is very important to me on a personal level. But I am also aware that there is an effort going on in society to understand what love is and what heart is — what it would mean for the world if we all engage in relationships from the heart. While I don't have all the answers, I would offer that heart wisdom is different from head knowledge. As we learn the lessons that only the heart can teach, our perspective shifts to encompass a greater reality, bringing grace into our lives.

I have a colleague who identifies her goal in life as being a "heartist." A worthy goal for any of us today! Western society is consumed with problem solving, long-term planning, and heightened time efficiency. We prioritize the cognitive process to analyze ourselves and others. While there is nothing wrong with this — cognition has certainly served us well in many ways — the heart has information for us as well. Our head allows us to access information rationally. Through our heart, we access trans-rationally. The capacity to be open to and engage in the trans-rational is essential to living a full life. The two — head and heart — must function in balanced harmony.

To understand this idea we have to put our head knowledge into context. We are part of the Cartesian age of industrialization and mathematical excellence. We've been part of a philosophical evolution that has appreciated the mechanical, the logical. In addition, our modern era has brought a focus on individuality and a strong need to honor the individual. A person working from the head, this philosophy maintains, thinks of his or her own self-interest, how to self-protect, how to become the best individual possible. I think our use of logical instincts and societal training to protect our sense of self, our personhood, is ingrained in many of us. While this process of individuating has been one of the most exciting developments in the last two centuries, if we are exclusively cognitive, then the feelings — the heart — shut down. We run into the danger of shrinking down toward a one-dimensional way of life — instead of honoring our multi-dimensional reality.

"I know the words but I don't yet know the tune" is the plight bemoaned by some of my friends who have achieved their educational goals, amassed plenty of material goods, and have challenging careers, yet still feel empty in life. This saying sums up the difference between living a life in which the heart is involved and one in which the heart is closed. You can't "know the tune" if you aren't engaged in the full rhythm of life. For the tune of life is embedded in the heart. It is the heart that stirs our melody of joy.

And it is Delores Williams, a feminist theologian who

represents a womanist perspective, who clarifies that in the black church, it is not the sermon but the singing that moves the spirit from person to person, galvanizing the congregation. She and other feminist theologians recognize the need to move away from the intellect, so as to develop a greater openness to that part of us that is translogical. It is from this place that the heart truly speaks to us.

We are all a part of this large, worldwide human family here on earth. As with ripples in a pond, all we do affects not only those immediately in our lives, but all other life on earth. This may be why another feminist theologian, Carter Heyward, speaks of her understanding of upholders of the Judeo-Christian heritage being challenged to band together as "justice-seeking friends" searching for a "right relationship" with others in the world. Martin Buber spoke of the sacred being manifest when a relationship shifted from an "I /it" to an "I /thou," in which the other was held in esteem equal to the concern about oneself. Those who live from the heart do so contextually, focusing not only on the individual but on the collective as well. Living from the heart offers the ability to look into another's eyes, see into his or her life, so as to cultivate an understanding of what it's like to walk in his or her shoes.

"Heartists" are also aware of the ripple effect of present behaviors on the future. Within certain Native American traditions, the seventh generation policy is used in all decision making. Instead of thinking only for today, they base decisions on the impact those decisions will have on the next seven generations. Sensing the future in this way requires awareness of our interconnectivity and the capacity for empathy. A person who is functioning from the heart assesses problems with an eye focused not only on the individual but also on what is best for the collective.

Empathy cannot happen from the mind. It is a pure heart function. Often it is the proverbial breaking of the heart that ushers in the powerful onset of empathy. Though pain may crack the heart open — leaving us raw — rather than taking something away from us, it offers us a chance to be present to our own life process, to feel the heart stirrings — even though there is pain. As my friend Sara says, "The only thing wrong with pain is when we run from it."

A commitment of love that invited me into my heart was a story told to me by a Santa Fe artist, Dominique Muzart. She and a group of friends were concerned about pollution of the Rio Grande. So they created — from their heart and their faith — a ritual. Every morning they went down to the Rio Grande and took bits of trash out of the river, saying a Hail Mary as they lifted out each empty beer can or paper cup. They would meditate on the slow current in the river and say a prayer, visualizing the river as a large rosary. Each piece of trash, a bead.

I was moved when I heard that story. I was living in New York at the time, and had a fifteen-block walk from my apartment to my office. Usually, during that walk, I would be preparing to inundate my assistant, Elizabeth, with all the challenges we would be confronting that day. But after I heard this story, I began to shift my focus during my walk to work. I, too, would pick up pieces of trash, quietly offering a Hail Mary as I placed each piece in a city receptacle. By the time I'd arrived in my office twenty minutes later, I'd had all sorts of encounters with squirrels and dandelions (one of the few tenacious plants that struggle through the concrete cracks) as well as the occasional trash collector who offered a broad smile when he realized I was helping keep the city clean. Walking into my office, I felt grateful for the chance to live the hours in the day ahead. I felt connected to myself; and it was a process that transported me out of my head — that mighty list-making machine — and into a place that is difficult to articulate but offers such sustenance and nurturance for me. Such a simple ritual completely shifted my perspective for the rest of the day.

We all know exercise is good for us, but how easy is it to maintain a regimen? Similarly, though living from the heart offers rich rewards, this state is difficult to achieve and maintain. Looking at "family as a spiritual practice," we can reinterpret the dissension that inevitably erupts as an invitation to heart exercise. My husband, Harville, and I have a blended family, with kids ranging from age twenty-six to ten. We are blessed / cursed with the challenge of surviving all the developmental crises going on simultaneously! In a wild and woolly household, things can get quite chaotic. When frustrated with each other, Harville and I occasionally say, "Talk to me like I'm someone you love." This is a reminder that it is not just the content that gets conveyed but also the delivery. Can we talk in a way that invites the listening?

Genuine loving — a love that does not strive to change or to control — means actually caring for someone else's welfare as much as you care for your own. Genuine loving has the potential to be the woof and warp — the foundation — of our every interaction.

Pain is often the impetus that motivates us as we strive to open fully to ourselves, to others, and to life. Our spiritual practice can put both the pain and the capacity to love into a framework. The faith and the belief in rebirth and resurrection that is a part of my spiritual practice is my bedrock as I maneuver the currents of life — reminding me that there are continuous cycles. The concept of life, death, and resurrection is alive everywhere, and perhaps most profoundly felt in nature. The seasons come and go — winter following spring following winter. If we look at pain as being the "winter" of our lives, then the sure knowledge that we will again experience our own "spring" can help offer a larger perspective and allow us to cultivate the compassion and patience to await our personal thaw.

The heart grows when it is in covenant with someone else. While there is intimacy, there must also be boundaries. Anger, for example, is one face of love. Anger, so often seen as negative within our society, can be a cleansing force. It is crucial for us to understand the role of anger in moving into the heart. And dealing with anger — our own and others' — means setting and accepting limits. These limits, though initially they may not seem to, help us as we move toward genuine love.

We have to work on learning to make one another safe so that we can evolve and heartwork can happen. A clear standard is set in I John 4:18: "There is no fear in love; but perfect love casteth out fear." So genuine love has a lot to do with safety. Without clear boundaries, which act as a protection of the self, we do not feel comfortable opening up to intimacy. And it is empathy for one another's point of view that also aids us in feeling safe. As we work on our boundaries and empathy, we open to intimacy and experience genuine love.

That is where a spiritual practice comes in. Beyond the fractured nature of much of our lives and relationships, there is a unifying whole. Most scientists recognize that there is a higher intelligence in operation. Just developing a sense of that higher sphere can, I feel, help us minimize the fear we have of one another, the fear of making mistakes, the fear of our anger. Just as pain and anger help us in our growth, so too do mistakes. To assume that we can be perfect, or to attempt to strive toward perfection, is instantly demoralizing. Perfection is a goal that lies forever outside our grasp. Rather, we need to embrace our mistakes and learn from them. Each mistake can bring us closer to genuine love. And as the love grows, our lives grow — and we can live a life full and complete, thinking with our heads but living from our hearts.

A Mixture of Love

by *Shakti Gawain*

"I believe that, as eternal spiritual beings, we have taken physical form in order to experience a unique, amazing, and fantastic (although often difficult) journey as human beings. We are here to learn about both kinds of love: human love, with its needs and desires and inconsistencies, and spiritual love, with its all-encompassing benevolence."

I BELIEVE THAT there are two basic kinds of love: spiritual love and what I call "human love." Spiritual love manifests itself when we are deeply connected to our own essence (our spirit), to the life force and the oneness. It's a kind of open, expansive feeling of affiliation with all of life. It is unconditional love. Human love, on the other hand, involves our personal needs on physical, emotional, and mental levels. It's not unconditional love.

What we commonly refer to as "love" is usually a mixture of these two and appears in many different forms —

as the love between a parent and child, the love between friends, or the love between romantic partners. A lot of people (especially those who are spiritually inclined) focus on giving and receiving unconditional love, as if this is the purest and best form of love and as if human love were somehow inferior. But the truth of the matter is that we can only feel unconditional love when our physical, emotional, and mental needs have been met. Unconditional spiritual love is blocked when we are emotionally wounded, when we don't know how to take care of ourselves, or when we don't live by our own sense of truth. Only as we heal our emotional wounds and care for ourselves on all levels can we begin to experience truly unconditional love.

I believe that, as eternal spiritual beings, we have taken physical form in order to experience a unique, amazing, and fantastic (although often difficult) journey as human beings. We are here to learn about both kinds of love: human love, with its needs and desires and inconsistencies, and spiritual love, with its all-encompassing benevolence. Some people try to bypass the human experience. Thinking that human love is somehow less important or on a lower level, they attempt to directly access the "higher plane" of spiritual love. But we can't recognize and satisfy the needs of others until we learn how to recognize and satisfy our own human needs. We must learn to love ourselves, including the parts that we believe are bad. Too many people try to love without allowing themselves to experience "bad" feelings, such as anger, sadness, or selfishness. These people try to be continually happy, loving, and giving — denying that they have any negative feelings. But this approach never works, for whatever we reject about ourselves eventually comes back to claim us.

But if we can learn to accept — even love — our hatred, our dependency, our needs, and our fears as part of the human experience, we can extend this love and acceptance to another. This is true compassion. When this is achieved, we can more easily connect to the life force, to the universe, and to a truly spiritual kind of love. So, true spiritual love begins with learning to love and accept ourselves.

In order to truly love and care for ourselves, we must tune in to our own needs, feelings, and energies — we must "stay close to ourselves" as much as possible. The more we are able to do so, the more connected we feel to ourselves. This, in turn, makes it easier for us to connect to others and to receive their love. To contact our inner selves, we must have some time alone every day, quiet time when we can take a break from the world, to simply relax and let it all go. I try to meditate a little bit each morning, even if it's only for five or ten minutes, just to get myself centered. But what helps me the most is getting outside for a while. I'll take a short walk or just sit quietly under a shady tree. Experiencing nature plays a very important role in my feeling connected not only to myself but to a larger entity. It also helps me put myself and my problems into perspective. Just walking through a grove of trees or seeing the great blue expanse of the ocean or listening to the birds sing helps me to remember that my problems and my being are just tiny parts of a much greater scheme. That knowledge can be very calming and very nurturing.

Once we get in touch with ourselves, with our feelings, needs, and desires, it's important to find others with whom we can be completely honest. Love depends upon honesty and the feeling that it's okay (and desirable) to express fully what's going on inside. But, of course, the other side of the coin is that both parties need to be supportive listeners. All of us need to feel heard. That's why just listening in a nonjudgmental way may be one of the most loving acts any of us can perform. Listening to and sympathizing with the other person's experience, even if our own experience is different, is the cornerstone of a loving relationship. True intimacy is attained only when both people feel secure enough to open up and share the deepest parts of themselves — their hopes, dreams, fears, and hurts. But this security comes about only through acceptance — and acceptance of another comes about only through acceptance of oneself.

I believe an important part of our work as human beings is to find ways to reconnect with that fundamental love that is the life force. It's not so much that we need to "get" it. It's there and has always been there. But many of us have somehow become separated from this love and need to find a spiritual practice that can help us reconnect. Regaining this connection to spirituality is achieved in exactly the same way that we regain our connection to ourselves — through quiet time when we are alone, when we simply stop all the busyness and center ourselves. Spirituality is found within us, not without. It's really just our natural state. All we need to do is to find out what is blocking us from it, and then start the healing process. The first step involves contacting our deepest core, accepting it, and loving it. For some this contact is achieved through meditation. For others it may be going to church, spending time outside, listening to music, or painting a picture. It can be anything — whatever gives you that sense of profound connection with life. The next step is to take care of our own emotional needs, since the foundation of every kind of love is truly loving and caring for ourselves.

The more we take care of our human emotional needs, the more easily we are able to love others, and the more we become attuned to spiritual love.

If you are searching for ways to add more love to your life, begin with loving yourself. Love is not something that comes to you when you are trying to "make it happen." In fact, in many cases the more you try to love or be loved, the more elusive love becomes. Learn to accept and appreciate yourself, learn to love even your "unlovable" parts, and you will see that love just blossoms within you and around you.

LOVE IS A CHOICE

BY *Richard Carlson, Ph.D.*

"In the end, I think my greatest concerns will be, How much love did I have in my life? How did I share my love? Who loved me? Whom did I treasure? Whose lives did I impact? Did my life make a difference to someone else? How did I serve the world? I'm certain that my only concerns will be about how I did or did not fill my life with love."

MY NINETY-TWO-YEAR-OLD grandmother taught me, in her way, that love is all that truly matters and is the only real measure of our success as human beings. Grandma grew up in very difficult times, the only girl in a family of six men. The family lived in the middle of nowhere, and Grandma worked hard from the time she was very young. She survived the devastating depression of the 1930s and the grief of losing her two-year-old baby sister. Her experiences taught her to be tough and strong; her motto was "It's a good life if you don't weaken."

Although my sisters, cousins, and I all felt that Grandma loved us, I couldn't remember her ever directly telling us so. A few months before her death, though, that changed. She had lost almost all voluntary control of her body and could barely move, and she spent her days lying down with her eyes closed. I visited her, rubbing her back, sitting close to her. Grandma was so weak that she had to choose her words very carefully. And she used those precious words to tell me — not just once or twice, but frequently — how much she loved me. Her body was deteriorating, her possessions were of no further importance, her accomplishments seemed small, but she had one thing left that really mattered — love. In a life that was rapidly changing, love was the only constant force. Over and over she told me how much she loved us all, the whole family, naming us one by one. The love she shared was genuine and sweet; I'll never forget her words or the feeling behind them. On those last visits during her final days, I knew without doubt that her words of love meant more to me than anything else her life may have stood for.

What a gift she gave me! Sharing her loving last days taught me so much about life and love. I often think about how I will look back on my life, during my own last days. I know that I'll ask myself, "What was my life all about? What really mattered to me? What was I most proud of? How did I spend my time and energy? How will I be remembered?" I think of these questions now because, to borrow a phrase from Stephen Covey, I need to "begin with the end in mind." When I think this way, my goals — and my path to those goals — become so much clearer.

I doubt very much that when the time comes for me to die, I'll be saying to myself, "I wish I would have spent more time at the office" or "Darn it, I never did get my bank balance as high as I wanted to" or "If only I had taken one more stroke off my golf game or lost those five pounds, my life would have been complete." In the end, I think my greatest concerns will be, How much love did I have in my life? How did I share my love? Who loved me? Whom did I treasure? Whose lives did I impact? Did my life make a difference to someone else? How did I serve the world? I'm certain that my only concerns will be about how I did or did not fill my life with love.

Many of us say, quite sincerely, that love is the most important aspect of our lives. Even so, how often do we focus instead on other things — winning arguments, getting what we want, wishing people were different, collecting achievements, consuming, seeking gratification, even washing our cars? My best friend and coeditor of this book, Benjamin Shield, taught me an important lesson: "We vote with our actions." It's easy (and often tempting) to pay lip service to love, but the truest measure of our commitment to love lies in our actions. We may with good intentions say one thing, but do something entirely different. We say, "My family is the most important part of my life," yet we rarely find time to spend with them. Or we might talk year after year about the virtues of putting others first, fully intending to help someone, yet never actually getting to it.

The questions you need to ask yourself are: "Is my family really the most important part of my life?" "Do I really want to spend time volunteering?" If we want our love to flourish in our lives, we must make loving choices. And we have to remember that love is not just a noun but a verb as well. In reality, we do vote with our actions. True, loving choices require true, loving actions.

Over the years I have seen that the people who do make

these real choices to fill their lives with love end up, virtually always, having the most satisfying and meaningful lives. When they not only say, "My family is important," but also make time for their loved ones, they receive a great deal of personal nourishment. Likewise, someone who actually makes the call and begins volunteering finds that there is tremendous satisfaction in working to help others. There are other, subtler ways we can make active choices as well. Someone who receives criticism and, instead of reacting and striking back, learns to take it in stride, realizing that the critic probably doesn't have enough love in his or her own life, is living out his or her loving choices. We have dozens of chances, every day, to make loving choices — choices that translate into warm feelings, gratitude, acceptance, positive relationships, and hope.

Having said that, I have to add that, of course, making loving choices is easier said than done. We are constantly confronted with obstacles that don't seem to warrant such a response. It's easy to think, "I'll be loving when . . ." and you fill in the blank — when my children start behaving, when my spouse acts differently, when my bills are paid, when my work is more fun, when I get through this stressful time, and so forth. What really nurtures a loving life, though, is our willingness to remain in a loving space and to respond with love during these more difficult moments. It's easy to be loving when everything is going smoothly and people are acting loving toward you. It's something else entirely to feel love for others (or for life itself) when you're in the midst of chaos or when other people aren't acting as you would like — when you're being criticized, when people are making demands on your time, when you do something nice that isn't appreciated.

One of my greatest challenges is the way I respond to

my children when their behavior is less than I expect. When I'm super-busy, trying to get everything done, and the two of them are firing requests and questions at me, in between having their own conflicts, I often react to the frenzied feeling in the room and demand that my children "act more loving!" But how silly that must sound to a four-year-old and a six-year-old! My intention is to teach them to respond to life with love, yet my actions — the tone of my voice, my frustrated demeanor, my demanding, judgmental words — are anything but loving. Here, as in so many other instances in my life, I'm hoping, even demanding, that others act loving, yet I'm unwilling to make loving choices myself.

I can always rationalize my own unloving reactions and behavior, of course. I can easily convince myself that it's appropriate to be angry in a certain situation. And that may even be true. So I give myself the benefit of the doubt. Yet shouldn't I extend that same courtesy to others when they act less than loving toward me? After all, from the perspective of my six-year-old, her behavior and reactions are as justifiable as my own. In fact, she has informed me in no uncertain terms, "Daddy, my life is way harder than yours!" And, you know, she may be right. She has a four-year-old sister following her around the house, whether she likes it or not. She's confronted daily with demands to learn to read and write and all the other difficult challenges of first grade. She has adults telling her what to do all day long. She needs permission to spend time with her best friends, even to go out of the front yard. And on it goes. The same is true for my four-year-old. From her perspective, her problems seem just as compelling — and they are!

How can I expect and demand that my children be

loving if I can't or won't do so myself? Doesn't the message my children receive from my example conflict with what I'm trying to teach them? Wouldn't they be getting the message to "act loving when everything is perfect, but at all other times go crazy"? And would the second part of the message be that "while you're going crazy, get frustrated that the people around you aren't able to act loving"?

I'm not suggesting that it's possible, or even appropriate, to act loving all the time or that you should act loving when you don't feel loving. What I am saying is that love begins in our own hearts. It is a choice. In a very real sense, to fill your life with love, you need to see love as its own reward. Giving and receiving must be seen as two sides of the same coin, different aspects of the same energy. Truly, it feels just as good to respond with love as it does to receive love. It's more important to be love that it is to get love.

When I do manage to keep my bearings with my children during those difficult moments — when I am love as opposed to demanding love — I notice how peaceful I feel and how quickly the immediate situation resolves itself. It's in these moments that I feel most proud of myself, contented and grateful for the gift of love. If I remain in a loving space, even in the midst of chaos, my family usually adjusts to my more peaceful state. The same is true for my wife. More often than not, she's the one (not I) who keeps her perspective while the rest of us act out. As she remains calm, the rest of us eventually come around. Responding with love is a powerful medicine.

When we do face the difficult times, we need to remember that circumstances don't make a person, they reveal him or her. If someone criticizes me and I fight back, all this says about me is that I'm a person who needs to fight. Yes, once in a while we do need to fight. But if I want my life to be filled with love, it has to start with me. After all, love comes from within each of us and is directed outward. Likewise, if I judge someone, my judgment doesn't really say anything about the person I'm judging. It merely describes me as someone who needs to judge.

If I want a life filled with love, I can't wait for the world and all the people in it to conform to my wishes. Actually it is the other way around. The love I want begins with me. As I make loving choices and fill my life with love, I start to notice that the people around me are also more loving. Then I receive the love I need. It's a circle of love that begins with me.

My wife and I have just started a ritual with our children that has helped fill all our lives with more love. We pretend that we have invisible antennae that are on the lookout for love. We sit, sometimes as a family and sometimes individually, and ask questions of one another, such as, "What went right today?" "What was the most loving act that you witnessed?" "What was the most loving thing you did for someone else today?" These questions help us think about the importance of love and remind us that there is good in the world — if we look for it. As we consciously consider the love in our lives, reflecting on love and loving choices, our lives can't help but be filled with love. Love becomes a habit. If our attention is on what's wrong, that's what we notice. If our attention is on what's precious, that too is what we see. It's not always easy, but it is pretty simple.

In our own little way, each of us affects the world with every choice we make. Either we are part of the problem or we are part of the solution. We either bring more love into the world or we get in the way. Each choice that we make along the way becomes an important step on the path of love. When being a source of love is our top priority, life becomes a magnificent, love-filled journey to be treasured.

Afterword

*"The best and most beautiful things in the world cannot
be seen, nor touched . . . but are felt in the heart."*
— HELEN KELLER (1880–1968)

WE HOPE THAT this book has, in some way, inspired you to let more love into your life. The movement of one grain of sand, some believe, can affect the entire world. So too, the simple willingness to make love the foundation of our lives can begin to bring more love into our heart and, subsequently, into our world. A wonderful teacher affirmed that "the shortest distance between two points is an intention." Often a simple change of our intentions can create the beginning of a whole new life.

We live in a culture that tells us love is "out there" somewhere. If we earn the right income, drive the right automobile, have the right hairstyle, and wear the clothing that is in fashion, *then* we are worthy to find love or love finds us. In contrast, the contributors to this collection teach the simple, yet essential, understanding that love truly does originate from within. In truth, our ability to give and receive love is directly proportional to our ability to love ourselves. We alone have the opportunity as well as the responsibility to create the love we desire in our lives.

It is comforting to be reminded that we already possess the most essential aspects of love in our heart. Accessing this love is most often a process of letting go of those obstacles that block love's expression. If we let go of those personal "speed bumps" along our journey, such as fear and low self-esteem, and truly let love in, moment by moment, we are well along our path to having the love we desire.

However, our intentions must be coupled with action. Japanese philosopher Takuan Soho once said, "One may explain water, but the mouth will not become wet." To make the words of the contributors to this collection truly our own, we must actively "push the envelope" of our ability to love. We wouldn't expect our bodies to get stronger and healthier without stretching and exercising. In the same way, by integrating intention with action, we must exercise our souls and minds and hearts to bring love into our lives.

Don't forget that loving is a process that must be attended to if it is to grow and thrive. It is our hope that, as you finish this book, it becomes not an ending but a fresh beginning. You will doubtless find, as have we, that just when you feel you have reached your goal, life offers your next lesson — yet another opportunity to live even more from your heart. Ram Dass said, "The ultimate test of even the most enlightened gurus is when they go home and spend a weekend with their parents!"

We feel honored to be a part of this project. We have worked with some of the most inspiring, loving people we have ever known. It has also been our honor to have *you* as our reader. It's our wish that this book affect your life in a positive light. It has ours.

With respect,

BENJAMIN SHIELD, PH.D.
2118 Wilshire Boulevard, Suite 741
Santa Monica, CA 90403

RICHARD CARLSON, PH.D.
P.O. Box 1196
Orinda, CA 94563

About the
Contributors

Jean Shinoda Bolen, M.D.

Dr. Jean Shinoda Bolen is a psychiatrist, Jungian analyst in private practice, clinical professor of psychiatry at the University of California Medical Center in San Francisco, and internationally known lecturer. She is the author of *The Tao of Psychology*, *Goddesses in Everywoman*, *Gods in Everyman*, *Ring of Power*, and *Crossing to Avalon*. Dr. Bolen's latest book is *Close to the Bone: Life-threatening Illness and the Meaning of Life*.

She brings to all aspects of her work an emphasis on the quest for meaning and the need for a spiritual dimension in life, while also taking into account the powerful effects of archetypes within us and family and culture upon us. She appears in two widely acclaimed documentaries: *Goddess Remembered*, the first of the Canadian Film Board's trilogy on women's spirituality, and the Academy Award–winning antinuclear documentary *Women—For America, For the World*. Her words are published in many anthologies and recorded on many audiotapes. She lives in northern California, practices in San Francisco, and has a son and a daughter.

Joan Borysenko, Ph.D.

Joan Borysenko is a medical scientist, psychologist, and author whose vision is to reunite medicine, psychology, and spirituality in the service of personal and planetary healing. She is the author of the bestseller, *Minding the Body, Mending the Mind,* as well as *Guilt Is the Teacher, Love Is the Lesson; On Wings of Light; Meditations for Awakening the Source; Fire in the Soul: A New Psychology of Spiritual Optimism; Pocketful of Miracles*—a book of daily spiritual practice—and coauthor of *The Power of the Mind to Heal.*

Dr. Borysenko is cofounder and former director of the Mind/Body Clinic at New England Deaconess Hospital and was an instructor in medicine at the Harvard Medical School. She holds advanced degrees in cell biology and psychology.

NATHANIEL BRANDEN, PH.D.

The name Nathaniel Branden has become synonymous with the psychology of self-esteem, a field he pioneered over thirty years ago. He has done more, perhaps, than any other theorist to awaken America's consciousness to the importance of self-esteem to human well-being. He has been described as "the father of the self-esteem movement."

Dr. Branden is the author of fourteen books, with over 3 million copies in print. He lectures widely to professional and corporate groups. His books include *The Psychology of Self-Esteem, The Disowned Self, How to Raise Your Self-Esteem,* and *The Six Pillars of Self-Esteem.*

LEO BUSCAGLIA, PH.D.

Leo F. Buscaglia, Ph.D., has written thirteen books, most of which deal with the experience of love. At one time, five of his books appeared on the *New York Times* bestseller list concurrently. His first book, *LOVE,* has been a continual bestseller for twenty years. Over 18 million copies of his books are in circulation, and his work has been translated into seventeen languages.

Dr. Buscaglia continues to research, write, and lecture internationally. He is deeply involved in promoting the dynamics of giving and loving through his nonprofit Felice Foundation and his work with a myriad of philanthropic organizations.

Dr. Buscaglia lives and works in Nevada. He is professor-at-large at the University of Southern California, where he taught for nineteen years. It was here that his famous "love class" originated.

RICHARD CARLSON, PH.D.

Richard Carlson holds a Ph.D. in psychology and is a nationally known stress-management consultant and teacher in the field of personal development and happiness. For several years he wrote a newspaper column called "Prescriptions for Happiness," and he is the author of many popular books, including *Handbook for the Soul* (edited with Benjamin Shield), *You Can Feel Good Again, You Can Be Happy No Matter What,* and *Shortcut Through Therapy,* as well as the *New York Times* bestseller *Don't Sweat the Small Stuff.*

Dr. Carlson is a frequent lecturer and a popular talk-show guest, having appeared on such shows as the *Oprah Winfrey Show* and *Sally Jessy Raphael.* He is married and the father of two children. He lives in Martinez, California.

DEEPAK CHOPRA, M.D.

Dr. Chopra is an international expert in mind/body medicine. He travels widely to give lectures and seminars and has appeared on major television and radio shows throughout the world.

He is the author of fourteen books, including the runaway *New York Times* bestsellers *The Seven Spiritual Laws of Success* and *Ageless Body, Timeless Mind,* as well as *Creating*

Health, Return of the Rishi, Quantum Healing, Perfect Health, Unconditional Life, Creating Affluence, Perfect Weight, Restful Sleep, and *The Return of Merlin.* His books have been translated into more than twenty-five languages, and he has produced more than thirty audiotape series.

Deepak Chopra is the focus of a critically acclaimed PBS special "Body, Mind, and Soul: The Mystery and the Magic," which began airing as a PBS fund-raiser in the spring of 1995. To date, this show has been one of the most successful PBS fund-raisers in history.

Dr. Chopra has been named as one of America's Top Five Speakers of 1995 by Toastmasters International.

STEPHEN R. COVEY, PH.D.

Dr. Stephen R. Covey is founder and chairman of Covey Leadership Center, a seven-hundred-member international firm. Its mission is to empower people and organizations to significantly increase their performance capability in order to achieve worthwhile purposes through understanding and living Principle-Centered Leadership. He is also founder of the Institute for Principle-Centered Family Living, a nonprofit research and development group dedicated to transforming education and improving the quality of family and community life.

Dr. Covey has taught leadership principles and management skills for more than twenty-five years to leaders in business, government, and education. His consulting portfolio includes more than half the Fortune 500 companies, as well as thousands of midsized and smaller organizations.

Dr. Covey is the author of several books and numerous articles on leadership, personal and organizational effectiveness, and family and interpersonal relationships. His book *The Seven Habits of Highly Effective People* was a #1 *New*

York Times national bestseller, with more than 6 million copies sold. The book has been published in more than twenty-four languages. Other books include *Principle-Centered Leadership* and his latest bestselling book, *First Things First*. His leadership advisory magazine, *Executive Excellence,* is in its tenth year of publication.

BETTY EADIE

The daughter of a Sioux Native American mother, Betty Eadie is the seventh of ten children and was raised in rural Nebraska and on the Rosebud Indian Reservation in South Dakota. Ms. Eadie is the mother of eight children and the grandmother of eight.

At the age of thirty-one, Ms. Eadie was recovering in the hospital after surgery. She was expected to recover fully, but sudden complications arose and she died. Her near-death experience is considered one of the most amazing ever told. Ms. Eadie writes about her near-death experience in the book *Embraced by the Light,* which has sold over 4.5 million copies and was on the *New York Times* bestseller list for more than a year.

She has given hundreds of talks about her experiences and has made numerous television appearances in the United States and abroad. Ms. Eadie lives with her husband, Joe, in the Pacific Northwest.

SHAKTI GAWAIN

Shakti Gawain is a bestselling author and internationally renowned speaker/workshop leader in the world consciousness movement. *The Path of Transformation: How Healing Ourselves Can Change the World,* her newest book, is the latest in a distinguished publishing history in the human potential market, including *Creative Visualization* (more than

2 million copies in print), *Living in the Light* (more than 700,000 copies in print), *Return to the Garden,* and *Awakening.* She has helped thousands of people learn to develop and act on their own intuition and creativity.

She has appeared on such nationally syndicated shows as the *Oprah Winfrey Show, Good Morning America, Sonya Live* on CNN, *Larry King Show, Jim Bohannon Show, Leeza Show, America's Talking,* and *New Dimensions Radio.*

Ms. Gawain cofounded Nataraj Publishing with her husband, Jim Burns, and was cofounder of New World Library publishing company. She and her husband make their home in Mill Valley, California, and on the island of Kauai, Hawaii.

JOHN GRAY, PH.D.

John Gray, Ph.D., is the author of *What Your Mother Couldn't Tell You and Your Father Didn't Know, Mars and Venus in the Bedroom,* as well as the phenomenal bestseller *Men Are from Mars, Women Are from Venus,* which has sold over 3 million copies in the United States and is available in twenty-six languages around the world.

An internationally recognized expert in the fields of communication, relationships, and personal growth, Dr. Gray uniquely focuses on assisting men and woman in understanding, respecting, and appreciating their differences. For over twenty years, he has conducted public and private seminars for over 100,000 participants. In his highly acclaimed books and in his popular weekend seminar, "Men, Women, and Relationships," he entertains and inspires his audiences with practical insights and easy-to-use techniques that can be applied immediately to enrich relationships.

John Gray is a popular speaker on the national lecture circuit and has often appeared on television and radio programs to discuss his work. He has been interviewed on the *Oprah*

Winfrey Show, Donahue, Good Morning America, Eye to Eye with Connie Chung, CNBC, and CNN, as well as countless local television and radio programs across the country.

LOUISE L. HAY

Louise L. Hay is known as one of the founders of the self-help movement. Her bestselling first book, *Heal Your Body,* discusses the connection between mind and body. Her lectures and workshops include her healing techniques and positive philosophy and teach people how to create more of what they want in their lives, including more wellness in their bodies, minds, and spirits.

Louise Hay was able to put her philosophies into practice when she was diagnosed with cancer. After considering the alternatives to surgery and drugs, she developed an intensive program of affirmation, visualization, nutritional cleansing, and psychotherapy. Within six months she was completely healed of cancer.

In her 1980 *New York Times* bestseller, *You Can Heal Your Life,* she explains how our beliefs and ideas about ourselves are often the cause of our emotional problems and physical maladies and how, by using certain tools, we can change our thinking and our lives for the better. Over 3 million copies have been sold throughout the world.

In 1985 Ms. Hay began her famous AIDS support group, The Hayride, which soon had grown to a weekly gathering of eight hundred people. It was during this time that she wrote *The AIDS Book: Creating a Positive Approach,* based on her experiences with this powerful group.

She now heads Hay House, which publishes some of the most notable self-help authors of our time, and has established the Hay Foundation and the Louise L. Hay Charitable Fund, nonprofit organizations that support many diverse organizations, including those dealing with AIDS, battered women, and other disadvantaged individuals in our society.

Louise's most recent book, *Life!*, was published in 1995. Her monthly column, "Dear Louise," appears in over thirty world publications. She lives in San Diego, California, with three dogs, two rabbits, and a cat.

HARVILLE HENDRIX, PH.D.

Harville Hendrix, Ph.D., the founder and president of the Institute for Imago Relationship Therapy, is the author of the popularly acclaimed books *Getting the Love You Want: A Guide for Couples* and *Keeping the Love You Find: A Guide for Singles*. In addition, Harville and his wife, Helen Hunt, M.A., who has been his support in developing Imago Relationship Therapy, coauthored *The Couples Companion: Meditations and Exercises for Getting the Love You Want*. They also collaborated on *Getting the Love You Want: The Home Video*, for which Dr. Hendrix and Ms. Hunt were executive editor and executive producer, respectively. This award-winning series was introduced and endorsed by Oprah Winfrey when it aired on public television. A former professor at Southern Methodist University, he holds an M.A. and a Ph.D. in psychology and religion from the School of Divinity at the University of Chicago and a master of divinity from Union Theological Seminary in New York. He is a diplomate in the American Association of Pastoral Counselors and a member of the American Group Psychotherapy Association and the International Transactional Analysis Association. Harville Hendrix and Helen Hunt have six children.

HELEN HUNT, M.A.

Helen Hunt has worked within the secular women's movement for the past fifteen years. President of the Sister Fund, a women's fund whose mission is to empower women and girls socially, economically, politically, and spiritually, she has been instrumental in founding other women's organizations in New York and Dallas. Most recently, she has deepened her focus to include a spiritual component and has been taking courses in feminist theology at Union Theological Seminary in New York City. She is currently working on a study that she feels may unearth ways to wed the spiritual and secular as women globally band together to work toward dignity, equality, and justice. It is feminist theology, she feels, that will help usher in a focus on collectivity and interconnectivity, energies that are much needed within our world today. She currently lives in New Mexico with her husband, Harville Hendrix, and two of their six children.

BARRY NEIL KAUFMAN

Author, lecturer, and teacher, Barry Neil Kaufman is the cofounder and codirector of the Option Institute, a learning center in Sheffield, Massachusetts, that offers programs for those seeking to be happier, more effective, and more successful. The Option Institute assists people challenged by adversity, including families with "special" children, to find hopeful and loving solutions to their difficulties.

His book *Happiness Is a Choice,* a national bestseller, includes heartwarming stories of his twenty years' experience working with those challenged by adversity. His ninth book, *Son-Rise: The Miracle Continues,* was released in 1995. He is currently working on two additional books to be published in 1996: *A Sacred Dying* and *Outsmarting Your Karma (And Other Pre-Ordained Conditions).* Mr. Kaufman is the father of six children.

Samahria Lyte Kaufman

Samahria Lyte Kaufman has spent the last twenty years dedicating herself to the limitless possibilities that exist for each of us. It began when she and her husband, author Barry Neil Kaufman, began treating their own son from what professionals labeled the "incurable" illness of autism. This journey became the subject of a book and then an NBC-TV special movie presentation, *Son-Rise,* winning the Christopher Award and Humanitas Prize. In 1994 the book was updated in the publication of *Son-Rise: The Miracle Continues* (which contains the original story as well as the stories of five other families who used this method to heal their seemingly "hopeless" children). She also coauthored the book and screenplay *A Sacred Dying,* applying her work to the subject of death and dying. In 1983 Ms. Kaufman and her husband founded the Option Institute.

Daphne Rose Kingma

Daphne Rose Kingma is a poet, psychotherapist, and teacher of relationships who has been in private practice in Beverly Hills and Santa Barbara, California, for more than twenty-five years.

She is the author of *Coming Apart: Why Relationships End and How to Live Through the Ending of Yours; True Love: How to Make Your Relationship Sweeter, Deeper and More Passionate; A Garland of Love: Meditations on the Meaning and Magic of Love; Weddings from the Heart: Ceremonies for an Unforgettable Wedding;* the groundbreaking book on male psychology for women, *The Men We Never Knew: How to Deepen Your Relationship with the Man You Love;* and, most recently, *Heart and Soul: Living the Joy, Truth and Beauty of Your Intimate Relationship.*

Her books have been translated into nine languages. She

has lectured widely and is a frequent guest on the *Oprah Winfrey, Sally Jessy Raphael,* and *Donahue* shows.

JACK KORNFIELD, PH.D.

Jack Kornfield was trained as a Buddhist monk in Thailand, Burma, and India and has taught meditation worldwide since 1974. He is one of the key teachers to introduce Theravada Buddhist practice to the West. For many years his work has been focused on integrating and bringing alive the great Eastern spiritual teachings in an accessible way for Western students and Western society. He also holds a Ph.D. in clinical psychology. He is a husband, father, psychotherapist, and founding teacher of the Insight Meditation Society and the Spirit Rock Center (P.O. Box 909; Woodacre, CA 94973). His books include *A Path with Heart, Seeking the Heart of Wisdom, A Still Forest Pool,* and *Stories of the Spirit, Stories of the Heart.*

RABBI HAROLD KUSHNER, PH.D.

Harold Kushner is rabbi laureate of Temple Israel, Natick, Massachusetts, after serving that congregation for twenty-four years. He is best known for *When Bad Things Happen to Good People,* an international bestseller first published in 1981. The book has been translated into twelve languages and was selected by members of the Book-of-the-Month Club as one of the ten most influential books of recent years. He has also written *When All You've Ever Wanted Isn't Enough,* which was awarded the Christopher medal for its contribution to the exaltation of the human spirit, *When Children Ask about God, Who Needs God?, How Good Do We Have to Be?,* and *To Life!*

Rabbi Kushner was born in Brooklyn, New York, and graduated from Columbia University. He was ordained by the Jewish Theological Seminary in 1960 and awarded a doctoral degree in Bible by the seminary in 1972. He has five honorary doctorates, has studied at the Hebrew University in Jerusalem and the Harvard Divinity School, and has taught at Clark University in Worcester, Massachusetts, and the rabbinical school of the Jewish Theological Seminary.

STEPHEN AND ONDREA LEVINE

Stephen Levine edited the *San Francisco Oracle* in the late 1960s. After intense practice of mindfulness meditation under the tutelage of an American Buddhist monk, he edited the *Mindfulness Series* for Unity Press. He has written several books, including *Grist for the Mill* (with Ram Dass), *Who Dies?, Meetings at the Edge,* and *Healing into Life and Death.*

Ondrea Levine, along with her husband, codirected the Hanuman Foundation Dying Project. For the past twenty years, the Levines have worked with the terminally ill and those in crisis. Together they share a soul in the deep, high mountain woods of northern New Mexico. They write and teach and heal in tandem exploration. Their newest book, *Embracing the Beloved: Relationship as a Path of Awakening,* offers details of much of their ongoing process.

PATRICIA LOVE, ED.D.

Patricia Love, Ed.D., is licensed as a professional counselor and marriage and family therapist. She is a clinical member and approved supervisor in the American Association for Marriage and Family Therapy and the past president of the International Association for Marriage and Family Counselors. She has two books, *What to Do When a Parent's Love Rules Your Life* and *Hot Monogamy,* which she coauthored with Jo Robinson. Dr. Love has published several professional articles, has been interviewed by numerous popular magazines, and appears regularly on national talk shows. She is a master trainer and faculty member of the Institute for Imago Relationship Therapy founded by Harville Hendrix. She spends most of her professional time writing, speaking, and training. She is known for her down-to-earth style laced with humor and practical information. She lives in Austin, Texas, amid friends, family, and the lively Tejano culture.

VICTORIA MORAN

Victoria Moran is the author of several books, including *Shelter for the Spirit, Compassion the Ultimate Ethic,* and *The Love-Powered Diet.* Her articles have appeared in such publications as *Ladies' Home Journal, Vegetarian Times, New Age,* and *Creation Spirituality.* She has traveled extensively in India and Tibet and lectures throughout the United States on compassionate living and practical spirituality. She lives in Kansas City, Missouri.

HUGH AND GAYLE PRATHER

Hugh Prather is best known for his books such as *Notes to Myself, Notes on How to Live in the World . . . and Still Be Happy,* and *I Touch the Earth, the Earth Touches Me,* as well as many others. He has been called "an American Kahlil Gibran" by the *New York Times* and "one of the compelling, insightful, inspirational, spiritual authors of our times" by *New Realities* magazine. He is a father, minister, teacher, and therapist.

Gayle Prather is cofounder of the Santa Fe Grief Support Group, which has been developed to assist parents who have had children die. She is also the mother of three boys and has been the coauthor (with her husband, Hugh) of several books, including *A Book for Couples, Notes to Each Other,* and

I'll Never Leave You. He has written that "Gayle is simply the kindest, most egoless, most intuitive entity on the planet." Together they conduct nationwide workshops for couples. The Prathers live in Arizona.

RAM DASS

Ram Dass was born in 1931 as Richard Alpert. He studied psychology, specializing in human motivation and personality development. Ram Dass received an M.A. from Wesleyan and a Ph.D. from Stanford University. He served on the psychology faculties at Stanford, the University of California, and Harvard University.

In 1974 Ram Dass created the Hanuman Foundation in order to promulgate spiritual awareness and well-being for people living in Western cultures. The foundation developed the Living–Dying Project, designed to provide conscious care and support for the terminally ill and dying. It also developed the Prison-Ashram Project, designed to help prison inmates grow spiritually during their incarceration. Both projects now successfully carry on their work as independent nonprofit organizations.

Ram Dass has authored a number of spiritual and self-help books, including the classic *Be Here Now; The Only Dance There Is; Grist for the Mill* (with Stephen Levine); *Journey of Awakening: A Meditator's Guidebook; Miracle of Love: Stories of Neem Karoli Baba; How Can I Help?* (with Paul Gorman); and *Compassion in Action* (with Mirabai Bush).

In 1978 Ram Dass cofounded the Seva Foundation—an international service organization working on public health and social justice issues in communities throughout the world. His lectures and workshops have been a primary fund-raising and public relations source for Seva's activities.

Ram Dass continues to lecture and teach throughout the world on such topics as utilizing service to others as a spiritual path, aging and its awakening potential, the relationship of business and social responsibility, personal relationships, spiritual awakening and its techniques, and social activism. When not traveling, Ram Dass lives in San Anselmo, California.

JAMES AND SALLE MERRILL REDFIELD

James Redfield has pursued an interest in human potential for the past twenty years. He has received a B.A. in sociology and an M.Ed. in counseling. Mr. Redfield has had a fifteen-year career as a therapist with emotionally disturbed adolescents. He currently writes and lectures about the spiritual dimensions of human consciousness.

His first novel, *The Celestine Prophecy,* is a gripping adventure story full of intrigue, suspense, and revelation. In this story lies a compelling vision of the new spiritual understanding that is emerging in personal and global awareness. Currently, the hardcover edition of *The Celestine Prophecy* has 1.2 million copies in print and has been on the *New York Times* bestseller list for more than one hundred weeks, having reached #1. He has also published *The Celestine Prophecy: An Experiential Guide,* a workbook companion to *The Celestine Prophecy.* His latest bestseller, *The Tenth Insight,* was published in 1995.

In 1989, after a series of life-changing events, Salle Merrill Redfield began to experience a high degree of stress and anxiety. Already familiar with the comforting effects of meditation, she joined a meditation group and was soon asked to become the group's leader. This experience served as preparation for the group meditations Ms. Redfield would eventually lead in conjunction with her husband when they traveled throughout the world speaking about *The Celestine Prophecy.* The success of these group sessions inspired Ms. Redfield to record her meditations for the bestselling AudioBook *The Celestine Meditations* and to write her new book, *The Joy of Meditating.*

Salle Merrill Redfield currently lives in Alabama and Florida with her husband and is a regular contributor to *The Celestine Journal* newsletter.

JOHN ROBBINS

John Robbins is the author of the Pulitzer Prize–nominated international bestseller *Diet for a New America: How Your Food Choices Affect Your Health, Happiness, and the Future of Life on Earth* and *May All Be Fed: Diet for a New World.* Many of the nation's leading authorities on alternatives in health and ecology consider him to be one of the world's leading experts on the dietary link with the environment and health. His life and work have been featured in an hour-long PBS special, *Diet For a New America.*

Mr. Robbins has been a featured and keynote speaker at major conferences sponsored by Physicians for Social Responsibility, Beyond War, Oxfam, the Sierra Club, the Humane Society of the United States, the United Nations Environmental Program, UNICEF, and many other organizations dedicated to the public interest. He is the recipient of the 1994 Rachel Carson Award. When he spoke at the United Nations, he received a standing ovation.

The only son of the founder of the Baskin-Robbins ice cream empire, John Robbins walked away from a life of immense wealth to pursue "the dream of a society at peace with its conscience because it respects and lives in harmony with all life forms." John is the founder of the nonprofit EarthSave foundation, an organization that provides education and leadership for transition to more healthful and environmentally sound food choices, nonpolluting energy supplies, and a wiser use of natural resources.

GABRIELLE ROTH

Gabrielle Roth is the author of *Maps to Ecstasy,* founder of The Moving Center, artistic director of her theater company, The Mirrors and a former member of the Actor's Studio (Playwright & Director's Unit). Her evocative music albums, including *Tongues, Luna, Trance, Waves, Ritual, Bones, Initiation,* and *Totem,* are at the cutting edge of trance/dance music, and her revolutionary video, *The Wave,* has catalyzed people all over the world. Devoted to exploring and communicating the language of primal movement, ecstatic experience, and the journey of the soul, she currently resides in Manhattan, where she teaches experimental theater and trains others to use her methods in artistic, educational, and healing contexts.

SHARON SALZBERG

Sharon Salzberg has been practicing and studying in a variety of Buddhist traditions since 1970. She has trained with teachers from many countries, including India, Burma, Nepal, Bhutan, and Tibet. Since 1974 Sharon has been leading retreats worldwide. She teaches both intensive awareness practice and the profound cultivation of kindness and compassion.

Sharon is a cofounder and guiding teacher of the Insight Meditation Society in Barre, Massachusetts, devoted to offering meditation training in silent retreats of various lengths. She is also a cofounder of the integration of the Buddhist teachings into the modern world. She is the author of *Lovingkindness: The Revolutionary Art of Happiness.* The book is a guide to the specific practices taught by the Buddha for the cultivation of concentration, fearlessness, happiness, and a loving heart.

BENJAMIN SHIELD, PH.D.

Dr. Benjamin Shield is a therapist, educator, and lecturer practicing in Santa Monica, California, and teaches throughout the United States and Europe. He holds degrees in biochemistry and biology from the University of California, with advanced studies at the Boston University School of Medicine. His doctoral degree is in the field of health sciences.

His work focuses on the integration of body, mind, and soul, while helping individuals to reduce levels of pain and to access exceptional levels of emotional and physical choices in their lives. He believes that healing and spirituality share common denominators and are accessible to each of us. Benjamin Shield has been a frequent guest on television and radio talk shows.

He has authored numerous articles on psychology, healing, and spirituality. His most recent bestselling book, *Handbook for the Soul,* has been translated into numerous languages. His other books and tapes (also in collaboration with Richard Carlson) include *Healers on Healing, For the Love of God,* and *Sixty Minutes to Great Relationships.* Most recently, he was a featured guest on the BBC / Canadian TV series *Medicine or Magic?* and a contributing author to the book *Alternative Medicine.*

BERNIE SIEGEL, M.D.

Dr. Bernie Siegel began talking about patient empowerment and the choice to live fully and die in peace more than fifteen years ago. As a physician who has cared for and counseled thousands with life-threatening illnesses, Dr. Siegel, who prefers to be called Bernie, embraces a philosophy of living—and dying—that stands at the forefront of medical ethics.

In 1978 Bernie started Exceptional Cancer Patients, a specific form of individual and group therapy utilizing patients' dreams, drawings, and images. ECaP is based on "carefrontation," a loving, safe, therapeutic confrontation that facilitates personal change and healing. This experience led to his desire to make everyone aware of his or her own healing potential.

Just like his two previous bestsellers, *Love, Medicine and Miracles* and *Peace, Love and Healing,* the third of Bernie's ever-popular inspirational books, *How to Live between Office Visits: A Guide to Life, Love and Health,* breaks new ground in the art of healing.

The Siegel family lives in the New Haven, Connecticut, area. Bernie and his wife, Bobbie Siegel, have coauthored many articles and five children. The family has innumerable interests and pets. Their home resembles a cross between a family art gallery, a zoo, a museum, and an automobile repair shop.

ANDREW WEIL, M.D.

Dr. Andrew Weil is the author of six books, including the *New York Times* bestseller *Spontaneous Healing.* He is a graduate of Harvard Medical School and has worked for the National Institute of Mental Health. For fifteen years he was a research associate in ethnopharmacology at the Harvard Botanical Museum as a fellow of the Institute of Current World Affairs. He traveled extensively throughout the world collecting information about the medicinal properties of plants, altered states of consciousness, and healing. He is currently associate director of the Division of Social Perspectives in Medicine and director of the program in integrative medicine at the University of Arizona in Tucson, where he practices natural and preventive medicine.

JOHN WELWOOD, PH.D.

Dr. John Welwood is a clinical psychologist and psychotherapist in private practice. His books include *Awakening the Heart: East/West Approaches to Psychotherapy and the Healing Relationship, Challenge of the Heart: Love, Sex, and Intimacy in Changing Times,* and *Journey of the Heart: The Path of Conscious Love.* His most recent book is titled *Love and Awakening: Discovering the Sacred Path of Intimate Relationship.*

Dr. Welwood, along with his wife, Jennifer, conduct Journey of the Heart seminars based on the principles and practices of his books for individuals and couples who are interested in conscious relationships. The Welwoods live and work in the San Francisco Bay Area.

MARIANNE WILLIAMSON

Marianne Williamson is an internationally acclaimed author and lecturer. All three of her books—*A Return to Love, A Woman's Worth,* and *Illuminata*—have been #1 *New York Times* bestsellers.

Ms. Williamson has been lecturing professionally on spirituality and metaphysics since 1983, both in the United States and abroad. She has done extensive charitable organizing throughout the country in service to people with life-challenging illnesses.

CPSIA information can be obtained at www.ICGtesting.com
Printed in the USA
LVOW08s2343080514

385004LV00002B/219/P